HOLDING ON

HOLDING ON

ON
Impulses to Leave
and Strategies to Stay

S. MICHAEL WILCOX

DESERET
BOOK

To those who came before,

whose enduring power

transferred the gifts

Image credits:
page 6, Federica Grassi/Getty Images; page 14, Grisha Bruev/Shutterstock.com;
page 28, MilousSK/Shutterstock.com; page 52, KristiLinton/Getty Images;
page 64, jocic/Shutterstock.com; page 82, Sascha Burkard/Shutterstock.com;
page 94, Natalia Golovina/Shutterstock.com

Visit us at deseretbook.com

Library of Congress Cataloging-in-Publication Data

Names: Wilcox, S. Michael, author.
Title: Holding on : impulses to leave and strategies to stay / S. Michael Wilcox.
Description: Salt Lake City, Utah : Deseret Book, [2021] | Includes bibliographical
  references and index. | Summary: "Latter-day Saint scholar S. Michael Wilcox
  discusses those who leave the Church and those who stay and why"—Provided
  by publisher.
Identifiers: LCCN 2021003755 | ISBN 9781629729107 (trade paperback)
Subjects: LCSH: Mormons—Religious life. | Faith. | The Church of Jesus Christ
  of Latter-day Saints—Membership.
Classification: LCC BX8656 .W555 2021 | DDC 248.4/89332—dc23
LC record available at https://lccn.loc.gov/2021003755

Printed in the United States of America
PubLitho, Draper, UT

10   9   8   7   6   5   4   3   2

CONTENTS

WHEREFORE,

STAND YE IN HOLY PLACES,

AND BE NOT MOVED.

—Doctrine and Covenants 87:8

INVOCATION

In 1833, Arthur Hallam, a close, personal friend of Alfred Lord Tennyson, died in Vienna at the age of twenty-two. He was engaged to Tennyson's sister, Emily. His death profoundly touched the great poet, bringing to the surface feelings and questions that had long disturbed him. *Was the faith he grew up with really true?* He wrestled with the burgeoning observations of science that challenged centuries of religious thought. What role did God play? Was there life after death? Was there even a God? Could he trust those who professed religious truth? Among all the affirmations of faith, on which could he rely? Were they reality or illusions?

He poured out his grief, anguish, hopes, and doubts into verse, which he dedicated to his friend, calling it *In Memoriam.* Tennyson began the poem with a prayer, an appeal to his Savior—the best beginning for anyone troubled by people, an institution, principles, or experiences that interrupt the flourishing of faith.

> Strong Son of God, immortal Love,
> Whom we, that have not seen thy face,
> By faith, and faith alone, embrace,
> Believing where we cannot prove; . . .
>
> We have but faith: we cannot know;
> For knowledge is of things we see;
> And yet we trust it comes from thee,
> A beam in darkness: let it grow.
>
> ("Prologue," *In Memoriam*, lines 1–4; 21–24)

Faith is a growing thing, the "beam in darkness," dimming or brightening. As Alma so succinctly pointed out in his metaphorical masterpiece, faith is a seed from the tree of life, planted in the human heart and needing continual nourishment (see Alma 32:40–41). For us, faith centers on Jesus. Yet life's droughts, weeds, and wildfires *interrupt* the growing. If these are not challenging enough, there are *loggers* who come to deliberately cut it down.

Tennyson's pouring-out poem portrays the earnestness of his wrestling:

> I falter where I firmly trod,
> And falling with my weight of cares

Upon the great world's altar-stairs
That slope thro' darkness up to God,

I stretch lame hands of faith and grope,
And gather dust and chaff, and call
To what I feel is Lord of all,
And faintly trust the larger hope. . . .

O life as futile and as frail!
O for thy voice to soothe and bless!
What hope of answer, or redress?
Behind the veil, behind the veil.

(*In Memoriam*, LV, lines 13–20; LVI, lines 25–28)

I think of that father two thousand years ago, crying out in the agony of his soul to Jesus, "Lord, I believe; help thou mine unbelief" (Mark 9:24). We long for the soothing answers only God can give, to peek behind the veil. Tennyson won his battle—as much as one in mortality can triumph in matters of belief. Although most prefer to be Thomas and feel the prints of the nails "and be not faithless, but believing" (John 20:27), we gain depth and spiritual muscle when we are "perplext in faith" with "honest doubt" (*In Memoriam*, XCVI, lines 9, 11). We "fight the good fight of faith, lay hold on eternal life," as Paul wrote (1 Timothy 6:12). It is a combat and a gripping! We desire to prevail. It may be long and tiring. We strive to stand firm and "be not moved" (Doctrine and Covenants 87:8), to emerge stronger, assured God is with us in all moments of doubt, question, and fear. We hope Tennyson's words can truly be said of us. They voice my personal prayer:

> He fought his doubts and gather'd strength,
> He would not make his judgment blind,
> But faced the spectres of the mind
> And laid them; thus he came at length
>
> To find a stronger faith his own;
> And Power was with him in the night,
> Which makes the darkness and the light,
> And dwells not in the light alone.
>
> (*In Memoriam*, XCVI, lines 13–20)

CHAPTER ONE

HOLD ON

Shall we not go on in so great a cause?
Go forward and not backward.
Courage . . . and on, on to the victory!
Let your hearts rejoice, and be exceeding glad.
—Doctrine and Covenants 128:22

Praying through the Darkness

I remember vividly my first "faith crisis." I was four-teen or fifteen. It centered on my desire to receive for my-self, independent of my mother, a testimony of the Book of Mormon. Except for a period of rebellion when she left the moorings of her youth and wandered in the wilderness for a season, she was a believing, committed Latter-day Saint and the godliest woman I knew. The solid base of her faith was the Book of Mormon, which restored her to her roots and anchored her there for the rest of her life. I can't recall a day when I did not see that book lying on her bed

stand or on the lamp table next to her chair. I started reading the Book of Mormon fully expecting that its con-
cluding promise would be fulfilled in my life as it had been
in my mother's. I was filled with Alma's "desire to believe"
(Alma 32:27). I wanted my own tree.

To my distress, all was darkness. My soul filled with
doubt, creating deep anxiety. *What if it is not true?* I asked
myself. *Why can't I feel the peace and assured whisperings of
the Holy Ghost?*

It was summer, and I was working on my uncle's ranch
in Nevada. We took Sundays off, had our own church
meetings, and rested the remainder of the day. I would take
the Book of Mormon onto the lawn under the shade trees
and read. Sunday after Sunday the fear spread. I would go
into the willows by the river and plead with God to take
the doubts away and tell me what I longed to hear. I was
answered with silence! Then more silence and still silence!
I remember being bothered by certain words and names
like *Anti-Nephi-Lehis*, and this voice inside my head was
telling me Joseph Smith made it all up. I was terrified. I
couldn't talk to anyone. My mother was in California, and
I don't think I would have dared unveil my fears to her. I
didn't finish my reading that summer. Somewhere in Alma
the despair became great enough that I closed the book
and turned my thoughts to horses, baseball, and girls.

Had I been older, would things have turned out differently? Would I have followed the impulse to leave? I had friends who left at that age. Yet I could see my mother with her abiding love of the book that now sat in the bunkhouse unopened. I eventually returned to the Book of Mormon, but it would be another five years, on the brink of my mission, before I received the witness I desperately wanted that summer in Nevada.

I don't know why I had to go through that. Was it a lesson of endurance, of staying, of wanting something badly enough that you don't give up until you receive it? Perhaps it was God teaching me that sometimes we have to pray through the darkness before the pillar of light appears—pray to the edge of "despair"—to the "moment of great alarm" (Joseph Smith—History 1:16). That is the first great lesson of the Restoration! The young Joseph in the grove believed he would get an answer but instead was overcome with darkness. Yet he prayed through it—"exerting all my powers to call upon God to deliver me . . . , and at the very moment when I was ready to sink into despair . . . just at this moment of great alarm, I saw a pillar of light" (Joseph Smith—History 1:16). There is something good, necessary even, about exerting all our powers when surrounded by forces with "such an astonishing influence" (Joseph Smith—History 1:15). We pray through the darkness until the light appears. This has happened more than once in my life. Light lives in darkness!

Hinds' Feet on High Places

Sometimes the road of faith thins into precipices at the edges. The straight path narrows to barely a foothold. The pain of offenses and gravity of doubt pull at us. During these times of praying through darkness, we must simply hold on. When the boy of the grove became a man locked in Liberty Jail, he cried, "O God, where art thou?" "How long?" he asked. The Father's answer was, "Hold on thy way" (Doctrine and Covenants 121:1–2, 9). Through a life of persecution, betrayal, pain, accusation, the death of children, and tragic setbacks, Joseph always held on.

There is a little-known prophet in the Old Testament named Habakkuk. He faced a crisis of faith also and, with foreshadowing echoes of Liberty Jail, asked, "O Lord, how long shall I cry, and thou wilt not hear!" (Habakkuk 1:2). He was challenged by the age-old question of why an all-powerful, all-loving God allows the righteous to suffer at the hands of the wicked. Questioning the character and nature of God, Habakkuk was answered: "The just shall live by his faith" (Habakkuk 2:4). Living by faith requires patience. Relief will eventually come: "Though it tarry, wait for it; because it will surely come" (Habakkuk 2:3).

When your ledge of faith is reduced to toeholds, visualize the image used by Habakkuk at the end of his little book. Though reason for belief may diminish and doubt dominate, "the Lord God is my strength, and he will make my feet like hinds' feet, and he will make me to walk upon mine high places" (Habakkuk 3:19). The image is of a "hind," a deer or other hoofed animal, swiftly and securely walking upon narrow mountain trails. "High places" refers to the spiritual levels of our lives—the sacred places. On the cliffs of the Judean wilderness, a species of wild goat known as the ibex walks on the tiniest ledges. It is impressive watching them, and the words of Habakkuk enter my mind. In Glacier National Park I have hiked the high trails to watch through binoculars the mountain goats maneuver dangerous ridges and near ninety-degree slopes. In Italy, Alpine ibex climb along impossible, almost vertical ledges, licking the surface of the Cingino dam for nutrients and minerals needed to maintain their health. I fix these images in my mind when asked to live by faith and "tarry."

Habakkuk encourages us to live by whatever tiny lips of faith we have. Like the ibex, we need nutrients—spiritual nutrients that are found in "high places." We "hold on" until the path widens. I have learned that it always does. Borrowing from another metaphor, we cling to the iron rod through the mists when the tree is obscured. The scriptures have multiple examples of people who held on when circumstances and challenges to their faith could have tempted them into disbelief or bitterness. Think of Joseph sold into Egypt or the multiple expulsions of the Saints. Our love of Jesus can provide a particularly firm holding place. When we are struggling to hold on, when we can't seem to find our spiritual nutrients, we can focus on our love for Christ and the Father and Theirs for us. Their love is a firm holding place.

If those dark moments in the willows at my uncle's ranch were the first of my life, they were not the last. When my wife, my beautiful Laurie, died ten years ago, my path narrowed. Unease and hidden fears crept into my mind, troubling me when alone at night. All my hopes and happiness rested on the beliefs of my chosen religion and the path I had walked since childhood. They rested on temple ordinances, promises, and authority vested in a temple sealer. They rested on the assurances of life after death and an eternal family. Was there a Laurie? Was she still mine? Did Joseph Smith teach revealed truth when he introduced celestial marriage?

This is an ongoing battle. I pray through the darkness for the pillar of light. I pray for hind's feet to stay on those high places that promise eternal reunion and everlasting love. The rope of faith upon which I hang has knots in it to which I can cling, but the knots sometimes seem to unravel. When that happens, I have to hold on so very much tighter. I wish I could say these struggles with faith are all resolved, but I continue from time to time to wrestle with questions and anxieties. Yet I can testify that over time my path has widened, sometimes imperceptibly. Time has proved a healer and comforter. I do so desire complete resolution and believe it will come, but it may, for me, come in eternity.

Our paths do widen. Not always as soon as we hope, but they widen, and the climbing becomes easier. The knots re-form. When doubts or interruptions to your rejoicing come—hold on with your hind's feet. Grip tightly! Walk the high places. "Though it tarry, wait for it; because it will surely come." If nothing else, holding on allows time to draw upon strategies, images, and truths that help counter the impulses to leave.

CHAPTER TWO

IMPULSES TO LEAVE

Fear not, little flock; do good....
Look unto me in every thought;
doubt not, fear not.

—Doctrine and Covenants 6:34, 36

His Little Flock

So often conversations I have, in varied contexts, center on what many call a "crisis of faith and doubt" and what I call "impulses to leave." The word *crisis* can be a bit threatening, especially when questioning implies a lack of faith. Individual journeys of faith change over time and may become more difficult. By "impulses," I don't mean spontaneous or flighty decisions. Impulses can be sudden, strong urges or desires to act—they can be driving, motivating forces in the mind, heart, or soul or a change in momentum. Many who leave the Church have done so with great inner turmoil, grief, and introspection. Sometimes it is not a matter of belief but one of trust. They still love their Savior and are still part of His little flock. Their desires to be good and compassionate remain and often intensify.

These conversations are poignant. They weigh on me. I have had many such discussions over the years. Their remembrance is painful, especially when the person describes impulses to leave in a beloved child, spouse, longtime friend, or themselves. I have seen former colleagues who taught religion for many long years leave the faith they had loved and lived. I have seen beloved past students walk away from once-professed convictions. I have seen treasured friends and even former Church leaders torn by conflicting internal emotions. People close to me describe feeling "a numbness of soul" or "the relief of release."

I think of a friend asking with tears, "How do I align what I believe with what I feel?" I have talked with ward or stake members who are hurt, confused, angry, or feel their trust has been eroded. I have wept with those genuinely wounded by the insensitivity and misjudgments of others. It saddens me. I know of personal family members' questionings. I love all these dear people. Though our friendships continue strong, I miss the communion of fuller shared believing and am grateful when their commitment to Christ remains constant even when their affiliation with the Church I love is fading or has ended. I believe in their goodness. "We don't need saving! We're not lost!" they've often said to me. Indeed, it is our loss of them and their gifts, not their loss of us and all we profess, that pains me so.

These individuals all bring back memories of my own private grapplings with doubt, qualms, and disenchantments and the awareness that I will probably go to the grave facing the battlefront of personal faith's oppositions. I suppose there will always be interruptions and loggers to my growing tree and perhaps to yours. For some, these may even arise from the faithful ranks of the Church. That is part of the challenge of having a growing thing inside us. Faith is a tree, not a stone. Mine is planted in the soil of Jesus Christ and nourished by the institution we call The Church of Jesus Christ of Latter-Day Saints.

I wish I could talk with those wrestling, as did Tennyson, with some element of their testimony, encountering barriers in their faith journey, struggling with doubts and questions, or suffering from offenses and deep hurts. I would speak with those considering leaving or who already have left the Church and with those who love someone who fits the above descriptions. And I want to speak to all members of the Church who do not feel these things now but who may in some future time. I wish we could talk one-on-one. I want to converse personally, honestly, casually, without judgment, and with understanding.

I have no desire or intention of trying to explain, correct, counter, or offer apologetics to specific challenges to faith. This is not my purpose. Many such offerings are available by far greater minds than mine. If those explanations, clarifications, or interpretations do not lighten concerns, in all likelihood there is not much I could add. But I hope to be the type of person Albert Camus spoke of when talking of life's battles—people who "despite their personal afflictions . . . strive their utmost to be healers" (*The Plague* [New York: Vintage International, 1948], 308).

A Mortal Journey

Anxiety-causing events, positions, people, or imperfections in the Church's history, teachings, leaders, or scriptures have troubled more than a few individuals from the beginning of the Restoration. This is not new. They are elements of a mortal, ambiguous world, filled with human frailties and weaknesses. Can we acknowledge the imperfections while still seeing moments of true greatness, reflective insight, and profound understanding of truth and finding a way to live not only a good but a godly and fulfilled life? We don't want to exaggerate faults or evade them; take them out of context or ignore them; feed offenses and hurts or dismiss them as minor. Admitting there are annoying gnats, we still might see the grand vistas.

Religion of all denominations and types likes certainty—sureness. This it cannot always have. Yet it often claims certainty in almost all areas of human thought, which has led to some interesting positions as well as uncomfortable backtracking. We do the best we can with the certainties that are granted us by a gracious heaven. And they are many! We also practice humility when the lines are not as distinct and extend sincere empathy for the wounded soul. We are granted many "I knows," but the "I believes," the "I trusts," the "I hopes," and even the "I supposes" must not be discounted as displaying a lack of faith.

I have been calmed on many occasions when grappling with my own journey of faith by an observation by C. S. Lewis. Speaking of God, he said:

> For He seems to do nothing of Himself which He can possibly delegate to His creatures. He commands us to do slowly and blunderingly what He could do perfectly and in the twinkling of an eye. He allows us to neglect what He would have us do, or to fail. Perhaps we do not fully realize the problem, so to call it, of enabling finite free wills to co-exist with Omnipotence. It seems

to involve at every moment almost a sort of divine abdication. We are not mere recipients or spectators. We are either privileged to share in the game or compelled to collaborate in the work, "to wield our little tridents." Is this amazing process simply Creation going on before our eyes? This is how (no light matter) God makes something—indeed, makes gods—out of nothing" ("The Efficacy of Prayer," in *The World's Last Night and Other Essays* [New York: Harcourt, Brace and Company, 1952], 9).

It seems to me Lewis has hit the core of the problem. Spiritual maturity arises through understanding limitations, accommodating those limitations, yet having the courage to fight, aspire, forgive, risk, dream, love, and struggle upward; to reconcile the what-ifs and the if-onlys that can devour elements of our faith. Flawlessness and precise wisdom will forever elude us in this present realm. The greatness of God is His ability to do so much with the "yous" and "mes" of the world. His work is individual, not collective. He grants us space to become. Equally (and I fear I will be misunderstood), I believe He wants us to generously fill in where we or others fall short and on occasion remember things and people a little better than they were, or at least to measure them at their highest. To do so is part of a compassionate, wholesome response to humanity. This is how I view not only the faith that I espouse and its founder, but all of life. This is how I hope others will view me.

Impulses to Leave

I'd like to speak from the experiences of my own wrestlings and what I have learned from them. I was born with a believing heart. That was made known to me at age twelve in my patriarchal blessing. I was also born with a questioning mind. Sometimes my heart and my mind have interesting conversations, even arguments. Sometimes it is my heart that tells my brain, "You just have to trust me on this." And sometimes it is my mind that calms the heart and reasons away the fears. Did not Jesus ask us to serve Him with all of our hearts *and* minds? This balance between heart and intellect is described by Tennyson in another section of *In Memoriam*:

> If e'er when faith had fall'n asleep,
> I heard a voice, "Believe no more,". . .
>
> A warmth within the breast would melt
> The freezing reason's colder part. . . .
> [Then] the heart
> Stood up and answer'd, "I have felt."
>
> (*In Memoriam*, CXXIV, lines 9–10, 13–16)

I also fear we may be discussing these impulses to leave and the issues generating them so much that we may create the very problem we are trying to combat! The best counsel, perhaps, on some occasions is simply "Let it be." Yet, concerns are real and valid.

Many Latter-day Saints experience unease over certain episodes of Church history or the life of Joseph Smith; over past or present policies of the Church; over offenses given, whether intentional or not; or over blows to testimony delivered by the changing moral and political atmosphere of our day. Fears and doubts can come from the desire to balance empathy, sensitivity, fairness, and equality regarding LGBTQ issues with foundational beliefs of eternal increase and the commandment to multiply and replenish the earth. They come from issues and assertions related to the Book of Mormon or Pearl of Great Price; from weariness of trials or the sense that one can never measure up and therefore does not belong; from the disillusionment that inevitably comes from living with flawed but striving human beings; and from the sense that one is being judged and labeled.

I rarely hear of something troubling one's faith with which I am not familiar, usually because I understand their unease through experiences in my own life. One thing I have noticed gives me a degree of optimism—there isn't much new that hasn't been around for decades, even centuries, though perhaps some things are more widely known now. Numerous leaders of the early Church followed the impulse to leave, including the Three Witnesses and members of the first Quorum of the Twelve Apostles. Many returned later, but for some the decision became a permanent alienation. The impulses to leave are not new. With Nehor "bearing down against the church," many Nephites "withdrew themselves from among them" (Alma 1:3, 24). Even certain disciples of Jesus "walked no more with him" (John 6:66). And in the premortal life, the Father and hosts of heaven grieved at the fall of "an angel of God who was in authority. . . . The heavens wept over him—he was Lucifer, a son of the morning. And we beheld, and lo, he is fallen! Is fallen! Even a son of the morning!" (Doctrine and Covenants 76:25–26). We hear heaven's lamentation in the cadence of those verses.

In spite of the consistency throughout the ages, when personal foundations are undermined, it can wring the heart. And humanity being what it is, the likeliness of spiritual injuries through another's insensitivity will always be present. These instances require understanding and empathy. Questioning and facing doubts are not condemnable wrongs. In the long run they often bring greater conviction. George MacDonald, a nineteenth-century

Congregational minister I dearly love, taught that questions are often hammers that break the opaque windows of our lives to let in light. The very word *question* suggests a quest. We want it to be a quest for truth and goodness. It is a search, and searching is something we are commanded to do. Alma's invitation to the poor Zoramites to plant the seed of belief established this need when he said, "Even if ye can no more than *desire to believe,* let this desire work in you" (Alma 32:27, emphasis added).

"To Interrupt Their Rejoicings"

As we journey on the road of faith, we can take comfort in knowing that others face and have faced similar challenges. Jacob said of his encounter with Sherem, "He had hope to *shake me from the faith*" (Jacob 7:4, emphasis added). The high priest of Gideon asked Korihor, "Why do ye teach this people that there shall be no Christ, to *interrupt their rejoicings*?" (Alma 30:22, emphasis added). In the early church Paul pointed out, "There be some that *trouble* you" (Galatians 1:7, emphasis added). Oliver Cowdery spoke of a time when "naught but *fiction feeds* the many" (Joseph Smith—History 1:71, footnote, emphasis added). In these encounters the interrupting and troubling fiction came from individuals who deliberately set out to destroy faith—in the case of Sherem and Korihor, specifically belief in Christ. In addition to the stirrings of our own minds, conversations we have with others, or painful events, we may likewise face those who deliberately oppose cherished and long-held beliefs. They may be sincere in their efforts or have an agenda. This opposition arrives more frequently now that we live in an internet, blogging, podcasting, YouTubing, and social media world.

Why We May Feel Impulses to Leave

Loggers:	Those who deliberately try to weaken, destroy, or cut down the growing faith of another person. (See Alma 32)
Faith-shakers:	Fears or temptations that destabilize our beliefs. (See Jacob 7:4)
Interrupters to our rejoicings:	Anything that blocks us from feeling the peace and joy of the gospel. (See Alma 30:22)

Faith is a gift of the Spirit, like healing or discernment. I was raised by a mother who had this gift. She believed! She believed simply, clearly, and fully. She was not troubled by anything except her own desire to be a better person. When life handed our family challenges, she would say,

"We'll put it in the Lord's hands, and all will be well." I envied her. My gifts were different, as may be yours. I have had to grapple with faith-shakers, interrupting moments, and even individuals who desired to destroy my "rejoicings," which she never faced. And more than once a local leader has pushed me to the point of exasperation or inflicted real emotional pain.

In these times I fix in my mind images and phrases that counter fears or impulses to leave. I will share more on this and other strategies in the following chapters. When facing interruptions to your own rejoicing or confronting faith-shaking doubts, troubling questions, or purposeful loggers, I hope these approaches will be beneficial for you. Sometimes one of these is sufficient. Most often they work together. Occasionally, I need them all! They help me feel the peace Jesus desires for us when He said, "Fear not little flock. . . . Look unto me in every thought; doubt not, fear not" (Doctrine and Covenants 6:34, 36). Drawing upon these strategies can help us hold on. We turn to them now.

CHAPTER THREE

BALANCE THE SCALE

It is given unto you to judge . . . ;
and the way to judge is as plain,
that ye may know with a perfect
knowledge, as the daylight is from
the dark night. . . . It is of God.

—Moroni 7:15–16

When the Scale Dips

Of all the images and phrases that have seen me through the questionings and doubts, the interrupting and troubling, balancing the scale has served me best. Sometimes we "hold on" to give us time to balance the troubling with the good. I bought a brass antique balance scale to remind me of this necessity. When watching beloved fellow Saints follow the impulses to leave, I always hope that they have thought about the scale. I believe many have. Yet, for whatever reasons, remembered positives were insufficient. For those who haven't tried to balance the scale when leaving, I plead for spiritual honesty.

In 1834, Oliver Cowdery wrote of balancing the scale when relating the appearance of John the Baptist on the bank of the Susquehanna River and contemplating the days he and Joseph worked together translating the Book of Mormon. "Days never to be forgotten," Oliver called them—days that "awakened the utmost gratitude." He continued:

> Nor has this earth power to *give the joy*, to *bestow the peace*, or *comprehend the wisdom* which was contained in each sentence as they were delivered by the power of the Holy Spirit! Man may deceive his fellow-men, deception may follow deception . . . till naught but fiction feeds the many . . . ; but *one touch with the finger of his love*, yes, *one ray of glory from the upper world*, or *one word from the mouth of the Savior, from the bosom of eternity*, strikes it all into insignificance, and blots it forever from the mind. (Joseph Smith—History 1:71, footnote, emphasis added).

Oliver's experience taught him that deception, fiction, and so on can be balanced—even struck into insignificance—by touches of love, rays of glory, and words of the Savior.

When uncertainty, hesitations, or disbelief, caused by any number of reasons, are dropped on the scale of our faith, it can be devastating. The weights "against" can seem so overwhelming; the voice that whispers, "It is not true," so frightening. Some action or situation may weigh down one side of the scale, leading us to feel no longer "at home" in the institution of the Church. Then impulses-to-leave emotions stir as alarm, embitterment, or disconnection.

I know these emotions well from multiple experiences and conversations. Within the last month I have seen the faith scale of several people I know begin to tip. These are some of the weights that cause them concern: Blacks being denied temple blessings until 1978, multiple accounts of the First Vision, Pearl of Great Price facsimiles and Egyptology, LGBTQ issues, addresses by General Authorities, the withholding of the sacrament to those struggling with their sins, enforcement of the BYU Honor Code, Joseph Smith's plural marriages, DNA and the Book of Mormon, science and the existence of God, the absence of women or people of color in the leading quorums of the Church, an offending bishop, a painful encounter with a stake president and the withdrawal of a temple recommend, and the weariness and fatigue of recurring guilt. Those weighed down by these concerns are wonderful people whom I love dearly. Some struggle with only a single element of the above; others face various combinations.

When issues such as these begin to weigh down too heavily on one side of our scales, we must take a deep breath, think clearly, remember fully, and feel receptively. Then we start balancing the scale. In Oliver's words, we remember the weights on the believing, staying side—the touches of love, rays of glory, and words from the Savior. We ponder given joy, peace, and wisdom. These come throughout our lives, individualized, and in different ways. Among other things, we can remember past experiences and the spiritually defining moments of our lives. Remembering is one of God's greatest spiritual gifts.

Rays of Glory from Joseph

I have balanced the scale in my journey of faith with rays of glory that came from Joseph Smith—especially the overarching message of his life. Joseph described himself in the 1838 account of the First Vision as "an obscure boy . . . a boy of no consequence in the world" (Joseph Smith—History 1:22). He showed me that God speaks to obscure boys and girls—that He is a revealing God. Such was I—as obscure a boy as you could find. But all the Church voices I heard—from my mother, who taught me to pray, to conference talks; from youth leaders to primary choristers—affirmed this opening truth of the boy prophet. "Heavenly Father, are you really there? And do you hear and answer ev'ry child's prayer?" ("A Child's Prayer," *Children's Songbook*, no. 12).

Joseph said of that momentous spring morning, "If he gave wisdom to them that lacked wisdom . . . I might venture" (Joseph Smith—History 1:13). It is the bewildered boy searching for his God that draws Joseph Smith so deeply into my heart, more so than the mature prophet of Nauvoo. Over two centuries since the Sacred Grove, Joseph tells me, "You might venture too." He speaks this as a friend. Notice how freely we all refer to him simply as "Joseph." Harold Bloom, one of America's foremost literary critics and scholars, spoke of "Joseph Smith's heroic enterprise in lessening the distance between God and man" (*The American Religion* [New York: Chu Hartley Publishers, 1992], 108). Thus began a lifetime of talking with my Father in Heaven, sparked by a fourteen-year-old boy's prayer in 1820. Within those conversations, rays of glory enlighten, but what is most precious to me is the touch of love Joseph first felt in receiving the forgiveness he sought:

"I cried unto the Lord for mercy," Joseph wrote,

"for there was none else to whom I could go and obtain mercy." The Father's introductory words—"This is My Beloved Son. Hear Him!"—was an invitation to receive what the Son brings to all: *forgiveness.* "Joseph, my son, thy sins are forgiven thee" were the first words he heard. Joseph said of that moment of compassion, so universal in its application, "My soul was filled with love, and for many days I could rejoice with great joy" (1832 account). In his 1835 account, he said the experience "filled [him] with joy unspeakable" ("Joseph Smith's Accounts of the First Vision," josephsmithpapers.org). One confirmation of faith is accompanying love and joy. "Go to the Father," Joseph tells us. "Listen in your sacred groves. You will hear him say of his forgiving Son—'Hear Him!'" It is the initial invitation of our history, given by the Father Himself. The Restoration began with mercy that is offered to all obscure boys and girls.

His prayer answered, Joseph returned home and told his mother the most important eight words I believe he ever spoke. "All is well. . . . I have learned for myself" (Joseph Smith—History 1:20). Joseph's whole life teaches that we can learn for ourselves, that all can be well—that all *is* well. God is forgiving. God reveals. So many touches of love received from heaven are those of forgiveness. They often come when we least deserve them or when we are overly sensitive to our own unworthiness. At the tomb of Lazarus, Jesus offered a simple prayer: "Father, I thank thee that thou hast heard me. And I knew that thou hearest me always" (John 11:41–42). This is the answer to most prayers—just the knowledge we are heard, so that we might venture and learn for ourselves. Joseph kept asking and learning right to the doors of Carthage Jail. I know that prayer is taught by all faiths, but I learned it in this faith, from Joseph's experience, blessing my life again and again. The sincerity of Joseph Smith's account is beyond doubt. My mother, my wife, and many close friends have passed now, but one constant relationship of my life endures—the one with a Father in Heaven who listens and answers and forgives. I lay Joseph's truths on the scale.

Touches of Love

Touches of love come through things freely offered, such as patriarchal blessings. I think of the initial meeting between Nathanael and Jesus, when the Savior referred to something only Nathanael knew. "Whence knowest thou me?" Nathanael asked (John 1:48). Things proclaimed in patriarchal blessings can cause us also to ask, "Whence knowest thou me?" My daughter, at the time an insecure teenager, prior to receiving her blessing, silently prayed God would tell her He loved her. The opening sentence acknowledges her desire and offers the love. Little touches of love! I lay those on the scale. It isn't only touches of love in my own life I draw on; I place yours on the scale, and you can place mine. Alma reminded us, "Ye have the testimony of all these thy brethren" (Alma 30:44).

Touches of love come frequently within temple walls—with the encouragement to connect with ancestors, we may feel love beyond the veil. The temples of The Church of Jesus Christ of Latter-day Saints are unique in the Christian world. In the hearts of men and women of this faith is an innate belief, expectation, and hope that our loving earthly relationships will continue beyond this life. In this Latter-day Saints are not distinctive, but we have elevated the belief in eternal love to the highest ritual and ordinance of our faith, to our utmost aspiration—an everlasting family. I return in memory to July 19, 1972. I knelt at an altar in the Cardston Alberta Temple and looked across it into Laurie's eyes. The mirrors' reflections shone in them. I heard the expansive promises spoken by the sealer. I felt timelessness. God opened His celestial window enough for a touch of love and a ray of glory to stream down unveiled upon us. I have never been able to adequately describe that brief blink of eternity but found in C. S. Lewis a description that comes close. It gives me scale-balancing perspective.

Such a sweetness and power rolled about them and over them and entered them that they felt they had never really been happy or wise or good, or even alive and awake, before. And the memory of that moment stayed with them always, so that as long as they both lived, if ever they were sad or afraid or angry, the thought of all that golden goodness, and the feeling that it was still there, quite close, just around some corner or just behind some door, would come back and make them sure, deep down inside, that all was well. (*The Magician's Nephew* [New York: HarperCollins, 1983], 161)

I lay that sealing splendor on the scale. It alone, independent of any other weight, tips the scale down on the side of staying belief and faith. It was the supreme moment of my life, its summit, the best day to be alive. How can I leave that? If God gave me only this memory, I would have lived a fulfilled life—more than compensated for all the gratitude, service, and obedience I could offer in return.

Words from the Bosom of Eternity

Oliver's description mentioned the power of words "from the mouth of the Savior, from the bosom of eternity." As an English major I've loved reading all my life. Words! Their combinations, rhythms, and cadences, the ideas they teach, are some of the heaviest things I lay on the scale. When shown some critique of latter-day scripture, I usually don't attempt to counter the specific challenge. Better minds than mine are doing this. When fears arise, I pull my scale out and place on it beautiful, deep words from scripture. Just reading Luke, for example, brings Jesus into my soul instead of uncertainties. I hear Him say, "Look unto me in every thought; doubt not, fear not" (Doctrine and Covenants 6:36).

Many times, people bring challenges against scripture brought forth by Joseph Smith. But let me share with you some of the beautiful words of truth that come from the Savior through Joseph. From Liberty Jail, he wrote to the Saints gathering in Quincy, Illinois: "The things of God are of deep import, and time and experience, and careful and ponderous and solemn thoughts can only find them out, thy mind O Man, if thou wilt lead a soul into Salvation must stretch as High as the utmost Heavens, and search into and contemplate the darkest abyss, and [the broad] expanse of eternity. Thou must commune with God" ("History, 1838–1856, volume C-1 [2 November 1838–31 July 1842]," 904[b], josephsmith papers.org).

I think of these words and wonder if, perhaps, social media posts or random online searches are not the best places to obtain knowledge concerning the most important decisions of the soul and eternity. Time and experience and careful thought are needed. We recall Oliver's faith that words blot doubts from the mind and strike challenges to faith into insignificance.

I journey through the pages of the Book of Mormon, balancing the scale. I ponder the clear, symbolic, visual imagery of Lehi's dream in 1 Nephi 8—so much of life encompassed within a few verses. I think on the philosophical validity and doctrinal understanding of 2 Nephi 2—Lehi addresses existentialism, relativism, determinism, and epicureanism, among other philosophies, simply pointing out their deficiencies. Reading 2 Nephi 4, I draw in the emotional peace contained in the poetic power of Nephi's human lament that he is "encompassed about, because of the temptations and the sins which do so easily beset me" (v. 18). I sense the tenderness in Jacob 5 of the Father's and Son's love as they work in the vineyard, nourishing, grieving, and laboring. I enter the woods with Enos to pray and hear Alma the Younger poignantly wish he were an angel with God's eloquence. There is King Benjamin emphasizing gratitude, service, concern for the poor, and the mighty change of heart. I read the metaphorical description in Alma 32 of planting a seed, illustrating how to obtain and maintain a testimony. I learn to be a good parent from the mothers of the stripling warriors and from Alma teaching his sons in Alma 36–42. Third Nephi 17 paints the tender picture of Jesus encircling Himself with children. The list goes on and on!

I taught brilliant college students of every discipline for almost forty years and never met one who could in their early twenties begin to give humanity the variety, power, life-shaping stories, unique personalities, and truths that emanate from the Book of Mormon. Yet Joseph Smith was uneducated—he did not attend so much as elementary school. The words he brought forth in the Book of Mormon more than balance the faith-shakers or the objections of my interrupters.

I turn to the Doctrine and Covenants and Pearl of Great Price, finding scale-balancing beauty, goodness, and truth that invite "careful and ponderous and solemn thoughts." Sections 76, 88, and 93 present broad and expansive understanding of eternal themes of God's work with His children; God's response to Joseph's Liberty Jail letter in sections 121–122 offers counsel in time of trial as well as instruction on the proper way to lead, whether as parent, spouse, or secular or religious leader. I hear the joy-instilling great hymn of the Restoration in section 128, as sung by the Prophet, ensuring us that gladness and rejoicing are the proper responses to all that has been revealed (see vv. 19–23). I lay on the scale four great visions of the Pearl of Great Price: Moses's vision of God's Creation (Moses 1), Enoch's vision of the history of the world (Moses 7), Abraham's vision of the Plan of Salvation (Abraham 3), and the First Vision of Joseph Smith (Joseph Smith—History 1:14–20). God's poignant conversation with Enoch as He weeps over the earth, written when Joseph had just turned twenty-five, is sufficient to blot out a great amount of doubt, fear, and anxiety from my mind. It's a heavy weight!

I balance the scale with concise, simple phrases containing beautiful truths and insight:

"Worlds without number have I created."

—Moses 1:33

"This is my work and my glory."

—Moses 1: 39

"Men are, that they might have joy."

—2 Nephi 2:25

"Men should be anxiously engaged in a good cause."

—Doctrine and Covenants 58:27

"The worth of souls is great in the sight of God."

—Doctrine and Covenants 18:10

"When ye are in the service of your fellow beings
ye are only in the service of your God."

—Mosiah 2:17

"Wickedness never was happiness."

—Alma 41:10

"The glory of God is intelligence."

—Doctrine and Covenants 93:36

"I the Lord am bound when ye do what I say."

—Doctrine and Covenants 82:10

"Let virtue garnish thy thoughts unceasingly."

—Doctrine and Covenants 121:45

"All these things shall give thee experience."

—Doctrine and Covenants 122:7

I add a final truth, appropriate for faith-shaking concerns: "It must needs be, that there is an opposition in all things" (2 Nephi 2:11). We can pull such phrases from nearly every chapter of the Book of Mormon, Doctrine and Covenants, and Pearl of Great Price—tiny weights multiplied thousands of times.

We have only scratched the surface of words from the bosom of eternity. These thoughts were not written by a fraud, a deceiver, a charismatic. We can reject him, be apathetic about him, ignore him, denounce him, or let fear and doubt overcome us, but Joseph Smith did not give us the choice of simply writing him off because horses are mentioned in the Book of Mormon or because he was an amateur Egyptologist when working with the book of Abraham facsimiles.

In the early days of the Restoration, a hesitant Martin Harris wanted to view the plates to validate his faith. In what followed, the Lord revealed the necessity and power of words from the bosom of eternity. "If they will not believe my words, they would not believe you, my servant Joseph, if it were possible that you should show them all these things which I have committed to you" (Doctrine and Covenants 5:7). Joseph Smith the man is not the central, critical factor in faith, nor is the visual reality of sacred objects. It is the words he delivered! Our faith rises or falls on the *totality* of the words he gave us, the truths they reveal, the goodness they inspire. Joseph gave his life in Carthage for words! John Taylor wrote: "The reader in every nation will be reminded that the Book of Mormon, and this book of Doctrine and Covenants of the church, cost the best blood of the nineteenth century to bring them forth for the salvation of a ruined world" (Doctrine and Covenants 135:6). Place his words on your scale of faith and see if their weight and power do not overbalance the criticisms heaped upon him.

I return to Harold Bloom, who, though not a member of the Church, felt "one's dominant emotion towards [Joseph Smith] must be wonder. . . . So rich and varied a personality, so vital a spark of divinity, is almost beyond the limits of the human, as normally as we construe those limits. . . . He was an authentic religious genius" (*The American Religion* [New York: Chu Hartley Publishers, 1992], 129, 92).

October 1967

The Sixties were an interesting time to grow up. We were the "now" generation, blissfully caged in the present—self-consciously superior, self-indulgent, self-deceptive in assuming we were individuals while succumbing to a strong herd instinct, and intolerantly tolerant as we challenged and melted the ethical and moral ground beneath us. Sadly, I recognize many of my generation's characteristics among those in our new millennium. It was in 1962 when I received my patriarchal blessing. Alluding to the decade of my youth, it warned me to keep free and clean from the offenses of my generation, promising I would walk without fear. It spoke of dangerous circumstances. I was only twelve. In my naiveté I thought the fear referred to the bullying I was subject to, and the danger might be fighting in Vietnam or other physical situations. In time I realized there were spiritual fears and dangers that were more serious.

When I was seventeen, I attended a priesthood session of general conference in person for the first time. I waited in line and obtained a seat in the balcony of the Tabernacle. It was October 1967. President Hugh B. Brown, a counselor in the First Presidency, rose to speak. I sat crammed in the narrow benches of the balcony as ushers pushed more white-shirted boys and men inside. I remember only one moment of that evening—President Brown's talk concerning the dangers of the world and a coming battle. Toward the end he paused. Then looking up, he prayed for the young men listening—for me.

> O Father, bless these young men. . . . Let thy Spirit guide them. May it hover over them, shield and protect them against the wiles of the adversary. We realize, O Father, that they are fighting not against flesh and blood alone. They are fighting against enemies in high places. They are fighting against empires. They are fighting against organized sin, organized rebellion. They are fighting against riots and all manner of disobedience and lawlessness.

O Father, help these young men who are listening tonight, when they go home to get on their knees and commit themselves to thee; and then they may know, and I promise them in thy name that they will know, that with thy help they need not fear the future." (Hugh B. Brown, in Conference Report, October 1967, 115)

It was an electrifying ray-of-glory and touch-of-love moment. I thought if I looked up, I would see God standing above the pulpit. President Brown brought Him into the Tabernacle that night. It was a scale-balancing moment from a scale-balancing man. Few have lifted me that high, and I have enjoyed many beautiful moments in general conference. I did as he said. I went home, got on my knees, committed myself, and had a profound confirming experience. I balance the scale with decades of memories listening to inspiration, words from the bosom of eternity, flowing from the pulpit of the Tabernacle and Conference Center.

Since Laurie's passing, I return frequently for comfort to Elder Joseph B. Wirthlin's "Sunday Will Come" address from the October 2006 general conference. All these words lighten the fear-opposing side of my scale. If troubled by some counsel, decision, or position coming from leaders of the Church on any level, or by those who challenge them, find your Hugh B. Brown talks. Lay them on the scale. Never let it go unbalanced! Find those life-altering moments, doctrines, truths, people, words, touches, and rays whose beauty inspires and lifts and balances the scale.

Other Weights

There are other revealed weights brought through Joseph Smith that help me balance the opposing pressures on my scale. I lay on it an enduring inspired organization; an edifying women's society; the economic system we call consecration; emphasis on family; a positive view of the physical body and its ultimate perfection; the aspiration of creating a Zion people, with one heart and one mind; the clarification of many debated Christian doctrines; a focus on the beauty and wonder of God's creations that "please the eye . . . gladden the heart . . . and enliven the soul" (Doctrine and Covenants 59:18–19); the understanding that salvation comes by increasing knowledge, not only liberation from sin; and a strong encouragement for educating all people. All of these blessings are offered to the world through a voluntary, widespread missionary program.

I think of opportunities to serve in our lay-oriented, everyone-is-needed faith. In spite of self-flagellations we sometimes inflict for not rising as high as our expectations, the reaching has something wonderful about it, some-thing God takes into account. We are encouraged to grow, improve, leave the world better, contribute, remember who we are, and pursue excellence, virtue, goodness, and knowledge. Wallace Stegner wrote, "Largeness is a lifelong matter. You grow because you are not content not to. . . . You grow because you are a grower; you're large because you can't stand to be small" (*Crossing to Safety* [New York; Modern Library, 1987], xviii). Joseph Smith taught that this human desire for "largeness" comes from an everlast-ing, divine destiny as well as an infinite past. God's "work and [His] glory" is to bring this all to pass! He stretched the soul's parameters to immense distances. Humanity is inherently good, born innocent, and boundlessly perfect-ible with unlimited agency and potential. He made God more approachable, more human, and humankind more divine. I lay this on the scale.

I lay all the good, salt-of-the-earth, decent, godly people who dare to aspire to be called "Saints" on the scale. I've lived all my life among them. In spite of their (our) humanity, which sometimes inflicts pain, they are overall splendidly wonderful—giving, self-sacrificing, kind, yearn-ing for higher things and higher selves, truly wanting to be all the thirteenth article of faith invites them to be, and even embodying it in those small moments of greatness that define character so thoroughly. The Latter-day Saint people are the greatest legacy of the Prophet and the Church he bequeathed to the world. He created a "people"—a community transcending nationality—as well as a religious faith (see Richard Bushman, *Rough Stone Rolling* [New York; Knopf, 2005]). "Ye shall know them by their fruits. Do men gather grapes of thorns, or figs of thistles?" (Matthew 7:16) When doubts surface, I look around me each Sunday, and these ever-striving "grapes and figs" people help to balance my scale.

The Second Fear

When balancing the scale myself or with others, I ponder what I call the "Second Fear." It is an acronym: **f**ailure to **e**xplain **a**ll the **r**est! If the "First Fear" is the distress brought about by questions, faith-shaking, or interrupting, the second is a lack of desire or effort to balance the scale with all the positives. To be intellectually honest, since so much depends on our decisions, not only for us but also for our families and descendants, we must not engage the Second Fear. There is so much goodness in all the rest.

We may also render the acronym as **f**ailure to *examine* **a**ll the **r**est! Because we have joined or even grown up in the Church, we may feel we have already examined it. We may feel the acronym applies equally to the opposite side of the scale, and that would be correct. Deep balancing draws out poignant emotions. But when the impulses to leave are present, I beseech you, regardless of how you feel or what the outcome may eventually be, don't allow the explaining and examining of what you are leaving go undone, unbalanced, or unremembered when deciding whether to leave or "be not moved" (Doctrine and Covenants 87:8). I have a third meaning of the acronym: **f**orgive **e**veryone **a**ll the **r**est. To that idea we now turn.

CHAPTER FOUR

CELEBRATE THE GOOD— FORGIVE ALL THE REST

Shouldest not thou also have had
compassion on thy fellowservant,
even as I had pity on thee?

—Matthew 18:33

The Grace to Forgive

There is one overarching law I try hard to keep when-ever I look at another person, especially those in history whom I know only from the pages of a book—when I can't meet them face-to-face or know what is in their hearts. *Celebrate the good—forgive all the rest!* I admit there are things on the interrupting, faith-shaking, impulses-to-leave side of the scale that are difficult to balance even with the best efforts. Perhaps one is hurt and justified in that hurt. Yet we want eventually not only to balance the scale but also to remove the negative weights. We can't always do that, but I have learned forgiveness brings amazing equilibrium—it is an immense remover of weights, the ultimate balancer. This concept seems most obvious, but it can be difficult in practice.

Forgiveness presents dilemmas for many Latter-day Saints. It carries implications and admissions. For example, we dearly value revelation and how it guides the Church, yet it can be more than challenging to admit, recognize, acknowledge, concede, understand, accept, grant, appreciate—choose your word—the *humanness* of seers whom God calls to guide His people, let alone local leaders. We may feel that a particular person or doctrine or Church procedure was or is mistaken, unjust, insensitive, unwise, imprudent, wrong, too traditional, or wide of the mark. Again, choose your descriptor. In these times, can we celebrate the good and forgive all the rest? It is helpful to realize that what troubles me individually does not give unrest to everyone. We may think it should, but personal uncertainties may not be universal.

Wallace Stegner wrote a novel titled *Crossing to Safety*, wherein we meet Charity Lang, a strong-willed, remarkable, generous, selfless, and loving woman who has only one flaw—the inclination to run everyone's lives. The habit is simply out of her power. Charity's best friend, Sally, makes the following observation that Stegner repeats more than once in the story. It's an enlightened admission about human affairs. "I'm ashamed. . . . I let myself get irritated at her way of taking charge of everything. I thought she was a tyrant to all of you in the family. I still do. But I shouldn't have ever let myself forget what a wonderful unselfish friend she has been. *I should have had the grace to forgive what I knew she couldn't help*" (*Crossing to Safety* [New York: Modern Library, 1987], 236, emphasis added). Remember the good, with grace to forgive all else!

I will share with you a memory regarding an issue whose weight has pressed on the fear, unease, faith-shaking side of my scale for decades. I was a junior in high school. It was 1965, the height of the Civil Rights movement. In a typing class I sat next to Linda Johnson, a Black student. We became friends. I enjoyed our conversations, usually conducted without the teacher's awareness by typing messages to each other while allegedly practicing. One day the subject of our conversation centered on religion. I don't remember all the back-and-forth. I don't remember what sparked her final question about my faith's policy regarding Black members; I only remember the numbing confusion and embarrassment as I read her typed words, "Is it because I am Black?" I typed nothing in response, just stared at her six words and the emptiness of my own page. How could I answer when I did not understand?

Years after my typing class, after 1978, I had another

conversation with a Black member of the Church. I love this woman. She has a bright, positive view about everything. Her insights are always welcome to me. We talked of Brigham Young and the decades-old policy toward Black members. That they had not been allowed to be sealed as families in the temple was most distressing for me. I asked her how she dealt with this and remained strong, how she joined the Church knowing that was there. She answered, "It was difficult, but I recognize Brigham Young, those of his generation, and following ones saw things through the lens of their culture. The most dominant social, economic, religious, and political issue in American history involves race. I still love Brigham Young. What would the Church have done without him?" She then added, "It was discrimination! I don't try to explain it or justify it. I just forgive and move on!" There is a level of spiritual maturity in her thoughts that seem to mirror so much of what the Savior spent His life trying to teach us.

I acknowledge that I am white, and the personal anguish the priesthood ban has caused and continues to cause for people of color is real and essentially impossible for me to comprehend, but if forgiveness cannot heal these wounds, I know of nothing else that can. Forgiveness can be very difficult for many of us, especially those with deep and accumulated injustices. Having empathy for all our brothers and sisters is paramount to our being able to embrace them and comprehend their experiences, as we strive to "bear one another's burdens that they may be light" and "mourn with those that mourn" (Mosiah 18:8–9).

I believe my friend was saying what Stegner meant. We must not forget the wonderful things—the unselfish, courageous, and inspired things. We can pray for grace to forgive what others sometimes can't help. We are mortal! I believe firmly we have power to personally remove many weights through forgiveness. I sincerely wish we didn't have this racial discrimination in Church history. I wish we had continued on the more racially inclusive track Joseph Smith had started. I wish we had led in the area of racial tolerance and equality. I wish we had been better healers of the nation's wounds. I wish God had come down in person and told Brigham Young: "No you can't say this! You can't do this!"

Were the assumptions and atmosphere of the times perhaps too strong a tide to swim against? I don't know. I have to admit that had I been born in the nineteenth century, I might not have been troubled by the policy, at least not to the level I am in our current century. That is painful to admit. The policy certainly was painful, and often overwhelming, for those who were Black and continues to be so for many today. We are products of our culture and times as much as we wish we weren't or fail to realize we are. That doesn't mean we have to excuse injustices of the past or ignore the pain that people felt, but we can move forward, working to make things better and using forgiveness and grace to prevent these concerns from hampering our spiritual growth. God works through agents, giving them wide latitude, as C. S. Lewis taught when he said, "He allows us to neglect what he would have us do, or to fail" ("The Efficacy of Prayer," 9). And so we pray for grace to forgive what others, even those called of God, understood or did. We pray for grace to remember all the good they did. This applies to everyone, now or in history, secular or religious.

Seeking Occasion

God knew these issues would arise, that members and critics would always be able to find, if they looked for them, imperfections and missteps. So He included in the Doctrine and Covenants His own feelings about such matters. Speaking of Joseph Smith, the Lord said, "There are those who have sought occasion against him without cause; nevertheless, he has sinned; but verily I say unto you, I, the Lord, forgive sins" (Doctrine and Covenants 64:6–7). This is a remarkable statement! If there were those in Kirtland who sought Joseph's faults "without cause,"

God gave them cause: "he has sinned." But God forgives and, therefore, expects us to do the same. "What is your problem?" I can hear Him say in a gentle, reproving way. Wisdom is recognizing what you need to allow. Although we shouldn't anticipate infallibility of the agents to whom the Lord has given the keys of His kingdom, we—both the faithful and the critic—sometimes do. One may not want to see fallibility; the other wants only to see it.

This view potentially disconnects us from the reality of human life. How do we reconcile leading by revelation with God-granted autonomy and human weakness? The very first section of the Doctrine and Covenants tells us the gospel will be "proclaimed by the *weak* and the simple." It reminds us God speaks and gives commandments "unto [His] servants in their *weakness,* after the manner of *their language.* . . . And inasmuch as they *erred* it might be made known; and inasmuch as they *sought instruction* they might be instructed; and inasmuch as they *sinned* they might be chastened, that *they might repent*; and inasmuch as they were humble they might be made strong and blessed from on high, and receive knowledge from time to time" (Doctrine and Covenants 1:23–28, emphasis added). Look at all those inasmuches! Look at the humanity and the Lord's understanding and accommodation of that humanity. We are all doing the best we can. If God forgives,

I suppose you and I ought to also. We are not asked to change our minds on these issues, but our hearts.

We try not to judge and condemn. The Lord releases us from judging. As an example—I don't know all the reasons for many of Joseph Smith's plural marriages. They are troubling to many, and I understand that unease. The concern can be a mist requiring us to cling tightly to the iron rod. It can require Habakkuk's "hinds' feet." I wish polygamy, like the priesthood restriction for Blacks, wasn't there. I won't know the answers until I meet Joseph and ask him. I've heard various explanations. Was it zeal to live a biblical life? Was it a desire to link himself to many of the families who supported and remained faithful to him? Was it a result of a still-developing comprehension of the sealing power? Was it to "raise up seed unto" the Lord? (Jacob 2:30). Was it the angel with the sword—God testing His people with a challenge as difficult as the one presented to Abraham and Isaac or Nephi and Laban? The Lord is still testing us, I might add! The early Saints wrestled long and hard in prayer over plural marriage. Have we? It is helpful to try to eliminate what it is not. I don't perceive the sensuality many attach to it, but I understand why that thought arises. But we may be doing ourselves, Joseph, and especially the women involved an injustice to linger there. Still, if we see error, we forgive, but we do more than that—we continue to celebrate the goodness.

Joseph once wrote, "We beseech of you, brethren, that you bear with those who do not feel themselves more worthy than yourselves, while we exhort one another to a reformation with one and all, both old and young, teachers and taught, both high and low, rich and poor, bond and free, male and female; let honesty, and sobriety, and candor, and solemnity, and virtue, and pureness, and meekness, and simplicity crown our heads in every place; and in fine, become as little children, without malice, guile or hypocrisy." Joseph included himself in that exhortation. He was trying. He spent his life, eventually giving it, endeavoring to lift the Saints every way he knew how, while dealing with his own imperfections and striving to comprehend "[the broad] expanse of eternity" ("History, 1838–1856, volume C-1 [2 November 1838–31 July 1842]," 904, 904[b], josephsmithpapers.org).

Wonder and Thanksgiving

I love Peter for his humanity. What's more important, Jesus loved Peter despite his three denials and other moments of weakness and short-sightedness. He was rebuked and corrected and forgiven. Yet God used him, and he rose to remarkable heights. I love Peter even though Paul had to correct him when he withdrew from the gentile Christian converts because of criticism from Jewish factions in the Church and undoubtedly his own ingrained disquiet over all things non-Jewish. Had Paul not been there, Peter's failure would have had catastrophic consequences for both Jewish and gentile members. Yet Peter was still the called and chosen leader, forgiven again and again. David wrote inspired psalms, beautiful in their love for God, and revered as scripture, even after his sins committed against Bathsheba and Uriah. We worship a forgiving God, a forgetting God, an "all his transgressions . . . shall not be mentioned" God (Ezekiel 18:22). In this may we follow Him!

Oliver Cowdery wrote, "I shall ever look upon . . . the Savior's goodness with wonder and thanksgiving while I am permitted to tarry; and in those mansions where perfection dwells and sin never comes, I hope to adore in that day which shall never cease" (Joseph Smith—History 1:71, footnote). Until that day comes, we can remove weights on the faith scale through forgiveness, difficult as it may be. This is what the Lord hopes we do with personal offenses. These come as we live, learn, and bump into each other. We wrong and bring pain into others' lives, intentionally or unintentionally.

It is hard not to feed those spiritual wounds. We are all

going to receive some. What will we do? In these cases, forgiveness may be the only thing we have to counter the impulses to leave. Then perhaps we will feel Oliver's wonder and thanksgiving. We will empathize with others trying to balance their own scale and may be carrying more burdensome weights. We will accept that we all are striving to please God as best we can, from the most senior apostle to the newest convert. There is room in the kingdom for all, those struggling with impulses to leave; those who, like a dear friend, say, "I'm here because I won't be driven away"; and those, like my mother, who just believe with simple, uncomplicated faith.

Balancing the scale of faith and celebrating the good while forgiving the rest is easier if we avoid a problem beautifully defined in a Danish fairy tale. We turn now to the problem of "mirror dust."

CHAPTER FIVE

WASH OUT
THE MIRROR DUST

I washed,
and do see.

—John 9:15

Andersen's Magic Mirror

In a prominent place in my house is a hand-painted, lacquer fairy tale box from Moscow. The painting on the outside depicts a fairy tale—not a Russian fairy tale but a Danish one by Hans Christian Andersen. Since Russian fairy tale boxes usually feature Russian stories, I was amazed at my good fortune to find one with one of my favorite Danish fairy tales. The miniature painting on the box illustrates Andersen's "The Snow Queen," which begins with one of his most powerful, creative images. The tale begins with a magic mirror, which has a devilish quality about it, having been created by an evil troll who Andersen tells us "was one of the worst of all, he was the Devil." Here is Andersen's description of the mirror's powers.

One day [the devil] was in a really good humor because he made a mirror that had the quality of making everything good and fair that was reflected in it dwindle to almost nothing, but whatever was worthless and ugly stood out and grew even worse. . . . Everyone who went to the troll school—for he ran a school for trolls—spread the word that . . . for the first time . . . you could see how the world and mortals really looked. They ran about with the mirror, and at last there wasn't a land or a person that hadn't been distorted in it.

Eventually the mirror was shattered and broke into a hundred million billion—and even more—fragments. And now it did much greater harm than before, for some of the fragments were scarcely bigger than a grain of sand; and these flew about in the wide world, and wherever they got into someone's eyes they remained there; and then these people saw everything wrong or had eyes only for what was bad with a thing—for each tiny particle of the mirror had retained the same power as the whole mirror. Some people even got a little fragment of the mirror in their hearts, and this was quite horrible—the heart became just like a lump of ice. . . . The Evil one laughed until he split his sides. . . . But outside tiny fragments of glass were still flying about in the air. (*Andersen's Fairy Tales* [New York: Signet Classics, 1987], 148–49)

I wish I could say I was immune from these fragments, but unfortunately there is a tendency in human beings to see things through the mirror dust, focusing on negative qualities rather than positive. We need to replace the devil's mirror with God's mirror, which diminishes the ugly and the negative while enhancing the beautiful and positive. I'm confident our Father in Heaven sees us this way. We needn't deny that people, as well as organizations or even books of scripture, have weaknesses or failings. But we also don't want mirror dust enlarging them until that's all that fills our vision or we decide to purposefully look for flaws to justify initial judgments.

"Condemn Me Not"

Moroni knew the distorting power of mirror dust and was concerned all the good in the Book of Mormon would be diminished because of its imperfections. He readily acknowledged the imperfections were there, referring to them more than once. The last thing he wrote was the title page, which would be the first thing future readers would ponder. The final sentence says, "And now, if there are faults they are the mistakes of men; wherefore, condemn not the things of God." As we've seen, God works with men and women, and men and women are not faultless. Their mistakes may cause pain or raise doubts in spite of good intentions and a desire to follow the Spirit. We know this from our own attempts to live the best we can. With mirror dust in our eyes, we can peer at those faults until we see nothing else, eventually condemning good that truly originates from God. Moroni also wrote, "And if there be faults they be the faults of a man. But behold, we know no fault" (Mormon 8:17). I hear his earnest plea. "We did the best we could! There may be flaws. We weren't always aware of them. If we were, we would have corrected them." I sorrow when directed by someone struggling with faith to articles or websites that pile up problem after problem, magnifying fault after fault as though that is all there is.

Hans Christian Andersen suggests a larger danger. Viewing things or people constantly through mirror dust can lodge slivers in the heart. It then grows cold, insensitive to the warmth of the Spirit or the beauty of forgiveness. Nephi understood this, telling his brothers, "He hath spoken unto you in a still small voice, but ye were past feeling, that ye could not feel his words" (1 Nephi 17:45). Moroni suggests an alternative when we see flaws and errors inevitable in any human endeavor. He earnestly pleads, "Condemn me not because of mine imperfection, neither my father, because of his imperfection, neither them who have written before him; but rather give thanks unto God that he hath made manifest unto you our imperfections, that ye may learn to be more wise than we have been" (Mormon 9:31).

We learn! Gratitude instead of critique! Education rather than repudiation! As growing people, we hope others will not continually scrutinize us through the mirror's negative augmenting power. We sense how much our Father in Heaven values the soul's education if we ponder the loss of the 116 pages. God allowed sacred scripture to vanish forever because He respects agency and knew Joseph—and all of us through him—would gain experience, learning something valuable about life, trust, and obedience. This is a *living* Church, filled with *living* people and a *living* understanding of God's great work (see Doctrine and Covenants 1:30). Line upon line, precept upon precept, we grow as individuals and as a church. God knows that His children—if they are sincere, if they are trying, if they want to do right and think right—will prevail in time.

Abraham Lincoln was harried by many voices urging him in multiple directions during the Civil War and the fight to free the slaves. In the fall of 1862, he opened his heart regarding leadership's burden when so many were continually assessing his efforts, often quite harshly: "I am approached with the most opposite opinions and advice, and that by religious men, who are equally certain that they represent the Divine will. . . . I hope it will not be irreverent for me to say that if it is probable that God would reveal his will to others, on a point so connected with my duty, it might be supposed he would reveal it directly to me; for unless I am more deceived in myself than I often am, it is my earnest desire to know the will of Providence in this matter. *And if I can learn what it is I will do it*" (*The Living Lincoln: The Man and His Times, in His Own Words*, edited by Paul M. Angle and Earl Schenck Miers [New York: Barnes & Noble Books, 1955], 500–501, emphasis added). If this is the desire of a politician, how much more so of a prophet?

The most obvious example of mirror dust and sliver danger is found in the life of our Savior. Here was this most beautiful of people teaching and doing good, yet His opponents and critics perceived fault and evil in Him sufficient to warrant death in a most violent and painful manner—and they even mocked Him in His agony. Mirror dust and slivers! If one reads the Gospels with mirror-dust eyes, it is possible to find impulses-to-leave faults even in Christ. We don't want Pharisee eyes or hearts like the scribes. Jesus taught His followers not to look for motes in others' eyes. He does not say that the motes are not there—they are—but why should we focus on them to the diminishing of all other beauty? This is a sword that can cut both ways—those who have left the Church also hope their continued beauty and goodness, not just their doubts, will be seen. As we discussed in a previous chapter, it is better to forgive and channel our thoughts to that which is good, healing, and wholesome.

"I Washed and Received Sight"

There is a true story in the life of Jesus that amplifies Andersen's mirror-dust fairy tale. Everything Jesus did physically during His ministry was designed to show what He could do for all of us spiritually. This is especially true of His miracles. Passing a man born blind, He announced, "I am the light of the world," and then proceeded to heal the man in an interesting manner. "He spat on the ground, and made clay of the spittle, and he anointed the eyes of the blind man with the clay, and said unto him, Go, wash in the Pool of Siloam. . . . He went his way therefore, and washed, and came seeing." To those amazed at his new vision, he testified, "I went and washed, and I received sight" (John 9:5–7, 11). Why would Jesus anoint this man's eyes with clay? It endowed the healing with symbolic power, leaving a broader message. The clay signifies the things of the world. If we wash them from our eyes, we see things we have never perceived before or imagined. Remember this man was born blind. Everything he saw would have been a wonder for him. The Savior announced He was the light of the world before He made the clay. Light in the scriptures is almost always interchangeable with truth. Washing away the clay and cleaning the mirror dust out enables us to perceive truth and goodness more deeply.

This truth is presented in Enoch's life, which teaches a comforting lesson about seers: "And the Lord spake unto Enoch, and said unto him: Anoint thine eyes with clay, and wash them, and thou shalt see. And he did so. . . . And he beheld also things which were not visible to the natural eye; and from thenceforth came the saying abroad in the land: a seer hath the Lord raised up unto his people" (Moses 6:35–36). Washing away worldly things allows one to see what others who have not washed can't see. A seer is a *see-er*—one who sees. Enoch was poignantly aware of his weaknesses and wondered why God would choose him, yet he washed, and God made him His instrument.

I believe all seers, aware of their own shortcomings, wonder why they have been called, but they have one thing in common. They have sincerely tried to wash the clay, the mirror dust, off so they might see with spiritual rather than natural eyes. (We get some sense of what seers see in Moses 7, in which Enoch views God weeping over the world in one of the most sublime visions presented by Joseph Smith.) With natural eyes, with our vision somewhat hampered by the world's clay, we may not understand what a seer perceives. We read just a few verses later that "all men were offended because of" Enoch's teachings (Moses 6:37). So the invitation is given to cleanse the clay away, to wash the mirror dust out, to keep the slivers out of our hearts.

When We Are Our Own Interrupters

We have considered outside forces—people or events that create doubt, sparking the impulses to leave—but sometimes we are our own faith-shakers, the interrupters of our own rejoicing. Viewing ourselves through the mirror dust, we perceive our "wrongness" rather than our divine potential, our missing of the ideal rather than our striving for it. The bar of expectations is set pretty high in the Church. I admit, sometimes when general conference is over, I get a little down on myself. There seems so much to do and be, and I fall short so often. We look at other Saints who appear much further along the strait and narrow path and higher on the ladder, climbing to heaven. We turn mirror-dusted eyes onto ourselves, and as always, the magic mirror does its darkening work. Failings and sins are magnified, victories and sacrifices diminished. Feeling we don't belong anymore, we seek associations or environments less demanding. We ask ourselves if we can relate to these "Saints." Do they understand us, or we them? Do our crimson sins really become white as snow, or do we always remain a little pink?

I brought back from Bethlehem recently an olive-wood carving of David. Most often we visualize David as the strong, faith-filled, determined young shepherd boy, sling in hand, facing Goliath. This was my image for many years. But now another likeness of the Old Testament hero fills my vision. Perhaps it's linked to the fact I am older, but it is the mature David, the king with his harp, I think of now. The carving depicts a much older David pausing in a moment of psalm-composing reflection, his hand drawn momentarily from his harp, a somewhat concerned look on his face, with just a touch of sadness in his loving eyes. I relate to this man. I wonder what he's thinking when I look at it. He made his mistakes—grave, life-burdening mistakes—but he gave the world our image of Jesus Christ as the Good Shepherd.

David wanted to build a temple for the God he had always loved, in spite of his transgressions. God intended otherwise. Solomon, David's son, built it. On the day of its dedication, Solomon spoke of David's desire and the Lord's response to it.

> Blessed be the Lord God of Israel, which spake with his mouth unto David my father, and hath with his hand fulfilled it, saying, Since the day that I brought forth my people Israel out of Egypt, I chose no city out of all the tribes of Israel to build an house, that my name might be therein; but I chose David to be over my people Israel. And it was in the heart of David my father to build an house for the name of the Lord God of Israel. And the Lord said unto David my father, Whereas it was in thine heart to build an house unto my name, thou didst well that it was in thine heart. (1 Kings 8:15–18)

One month before his assassination in Memphis, Dr. Martin Luther King Jr. chose these verses as the text for a sermon he delivered in the Ebenezer Baptist Church in Atlanta, titled "Unfulfilled Dreams." I think he sensed his death drawing near and that he would not see his dream of racial equality in America fulfilled. But he drew from David's desire the deeply profound message about our shared dream of being better people, building temples of character out of our lives worthy of the Lord's presence.

Dr. King stated, "Each of you in some way, is building some kind of temple."

Just as David never saw his dream completed, I suppose we may come to the end of our lives feeling the divine discontent that we were not as good, as faithful, as kind, or as obedient as we wanted to be. "Well that is the story of life," Dr. King continued. "And the thing that makes me happy is that I can hear a voice crying through the vista of time, saying: 'It may not come today or it may not come tomorrow, but it is well that it is within thine heart. It's well that you are trying.'. . . In the final analysis, God does not judge us by the separate incidents or separate mistakes that we make, but by the total bent of our lives. God knows that his children are weak and they are frail."

Dr. King spoke of what we hope will be said about us as we strive to be the best people we can: "Isn't that a wonderful thing for somebody to say about you? 'He tried to be a good man. He tried to be a just man. He tried to be an honest man. His heart was in the right place.' And I can hear a voice saying, crying out through the eternities, 'I accept you. You are a recipient of my grace because it was in your heart. And it is so well that it was within thine heart" (*The Autobiography of Martin Luther King Jr.*, edited by Clayborne Carson [New York: Grand Central Publishing, 1998], 357–58).

Those are the thoughts I have as I look at the reflective olive-wood face of David in midpause. His expression suggests he understands. I like to think he was composing a specific psalm when I ponder the little statue. It is the 103rd Psalm, which contains the following words. "Bless the Lord, O my soul: and all that is within me, bless his holy name. Bless the Lord, O my soul, and forget not all his benefits. . . . For as the heaven is high above the earth, so great is his mercy toward them that fear him. As far as the east is from the west, so far hath he removed our transgressions from us. Like as a father pitieth his children, so the Lord pitieth them that fear him. For he knoweth our frame; he remembereth that we are dust" (vv. 1–2, 11–14).

God gives numerous gifts. One is the gift of being able to learn from and consecrate our failures, mistakes, and yes, even sins. The tree of knowledge of good and evil is there so we can experience both the positives and the negatives of life. We taste both. We have the gift of our shortcomings, inadequacies, deficiencies, and faults, which allow us to grow. As contradictory as it appears, we may need our human frailties to learn godliness. That is certainly not an invitation to go out and sin. If we could, we would all live just as purely as Jesus! It may sound truly strange, but I am grateful for my sins. By making me aware of my own need for repentance and mercy, they have made me more grateful, kinder, more empathetic, more deeply compassionate and merciful, more ready to listen. I ache over them just as much as anybody else, but God has turned even these into goodness. "And we know that all things work together for good to them that love God" (Romans 8:28). I don't know about you, but I am fairly certain I would have been a self-righteous, judgmental, disapproving, condemning prig without a knowledge of my own sins.

I remember how starkly William Faulkner's words struck me in *As I Lay Dying* when I first read them: "People to whom sin is just a matter of words, to them salvation is just words too" (*As I Lay Dying* [New York: Vintage Books, 1990], 176). I realize this can be read two ways: those who sin and don't care and so are not grateful for saving grace, and those who don't think they have any sins of real significance and, therefore, feel no deep love or gratitude for God's mercy. It is the second of these meanings Faulkner presents us.

One beautifully endearing scene in Luke is the sinful woman weeping at the feet of Jesus because "she loved much" (Luke 7:47). Rather than feel unworthy, distant and apart, guilt-ridden, or not as good as other Saints around us, let the tears of empathy, compassion, and understanding of the human condition cleanse away the mirror dust. Let us love much. Let not our own weaknesses interrupt our rejoicing in Christ and signal the impulses to leave, believing we will feel more comfortable with expectations that are not so difficult to attain. We have a yearning, hungering-and-thirsting-after-righteousness religion, but we worship a forgiving, understanding, and mercifully forgetting God. We turn outward. We learn humility. We learn to love God and Christ more deeply. We learn inclusiveness without condemnation or judgment. We help others overcome in the comfort of the accepting softness of our spirits.

"But I Chose David"

I sense another truth in the story of David's desire to build a temple that helps me understand how we are led by revelation—we are guided by seers who have washed the clay away and are striving, as Dr. King and Abraham Lincoln indicated, to do the very best they can in doing God's will. It is a thought I believe can help remove the mirror dust and slivers. Both in 2 Samuel, where David expresses his desire to build God a temple, and in Solomon's retelling of the story at its dedication, the Lord indicates *He never asked for a temple.* Since we are a temple-building people and the temple figures so large in Jewish history, this fact may seem strange. In 1 Samuel the Lord says, "Since the time that I brought up the children of Israel out of Egypt, even to this day, . . . spake I a word with any of the tribes of Israel, . . . saying, Why build ye not me an house of cedar?" He was content during all those years in which He had "not dwelt in any house . . . but have walked in a tent and in a tabernacle" (2 Samuel 7:6–7).

In Solomon's retelling of the story, the word *chose* plays an important role. The Lord says, "I *chose* no city . . . to build an house . . . ; but I *chose* David to be over my people Israel." And God accepted David's desire to build a temple: "Thou didst well that it was in thine heart" (1 Kings 8:16, 18, emphasis added). It was the *desire* that was critical, not necessarily the thing itself! God chose David, and David chose the temple.

I think this is how the Lord usually works with His people and church in any age. God chose Joseph Smith, and Joseph Smith's intentions and desires were accepted. I am comfortable with the relationship we see between God and David. I can certainly accept the idea the Lord directly revealed to Gordon B. Hinckley the need to build smaller temples, or to Thomas S. Monson to change the missionary ages, or to Russell M. Nelson to reduce meeting times from three to two hours and to emphasize ministering rather than home teaching. But I am equally comfortable that these leaders, counseling with others, chose to do these things. Their sincere desires, intentions, plans, goals, and changes centered on pleasing the Lord and strengthening the Saints and, thus, are acceptable. The Lord can say as He did centuries ago to David, "Thou didst well that it was in thine heart."

It is helpful for me to believe God gives some people like Moses, like the Buddha, and certainly like Jesus— the *gift of religion*. If so, Joseph Smith surely had it. Like a skillful artist with paint or marble or like an eminent author with themes, rhymes, and characters, God's chosen prophets draw on their rare and godly gift. Maintaining heaven's confidence, they bring into existence the rituals, organizations, words and worship, directions and order, and doctrinal insights to edify us and lift us into eternal life. I wish to see the workings of that gift, but I wish to see them through my own eyes, not through the distortions of the mirror dust or the clay of the world.

CHAPTER SIX

DRAW STRENGTH FROM THE CHAIN

I saw the hosts of the dead, both small and great.
And there were gathered together in one place
an innumerable company of the spirits of the just,
who had been faithful in the testimony of
Jesus while they lived in mortality.

—Doctrine and Covenants 138:11–12

Welding Links

In a letter Joseph Smith wrote, included in the Doctrine and Covenants, he spoke of establishing "a welding link . . . between the fathers and the children . . . for we without them cannot be made perfect." He taught that this "union" must be "whole and complete and perfect," a "welding together" (Doctrine and Covenants 128:18). The words *welding link* suggest a chain. Chains are strong things. They hold under great stress and pressure.

Years ago my children and I were performing baptisms

in the Jordan River Utah Temple on behalf of our ancestors. Mirrors covered the walls on each side of the font, and we could see eternal reflections trailing into infinite space. Looking down those long corridors of symbolic time, Joseph Smith's words "a welding link" entered my mind. As I pondered the bonds of "the fathers and the children," the Spirit whispered, "You are looking at the chain!" That thought gave me pause. I reflected on it for a long time. The images in the mirrors did look like a chain—each receding reflection another link. The first reflection behind me represented my parents, the next my grandparents, then my great-grandparents, and so on back through time.

Looking forward, the first reflection belonged to my children, then my grandchildren and great-grandchildren and so on to the last edge of future time. I noticed in both directions that I was in each reflected link. I was in my ancestors and in my descendants. My forebearers looking to the link where I was standing could see themselves in me as could my children looking back up the chain. I was in them. They were in me. We were one "whole and complete and perfect union," welded together. That moment in the temple was profound. I felt my ancestors' strength, faith, and convictions, their hopes and encouragement, their experiences and choices flowing down that corridor—through those links. Whether they had the full gospel light or not, they have passed down valuable gifts.

When the faith-shakers and interrupters of rejoicing come, when the logger's ax bites, or when the impulses to leave threaten me or those I love, I go to a sealing room in the temple. I look into the reflections in the mirrors and ponder the message of the chain. I hear past generations whisper to me, "Draw strength from us!" My child-heart turns to those fathers and mothers. And I hear the waiting generations pleading, "Don't break the chain! Pass on the gifts and the goodness!" Those stable, uplifting, and protecting perimeters—send them forward! My father-heart turns to the children. We fulfill both sides of that scriptural, spiritual equation. We are parent! We are child! Hearts turn in both directions. Many of you are the beginning of the gospel chain—the initial critical link. How much confidence the Father must have in you to place you in such a powerful, decisive, and significant position! We must remember that when we choose, we often choose for generations.

In section 86 of the Doctrine and Covenants, the Lord speaks of the privilege and necessity of passing on bestowed gifts. He talks particularly of priesthood, but His words apply to all gospel gifts. "Therefore, thus saith the Lord unto you, with whom the [gospel] hath continued through the lineage of your fathers—For ye are lawful heirs. . . . Therefore your life and the [gospel] have remained, *and must needs remain through you and your lineage*" (Doctrine and Covenants 86:8–10, emphasis added). This principle can be relevant to the many inheritances received from our ancestry and passed on to our descendants but applies here specifically to the truths of the Restoration.

The insights from section 86 can be helpful as we examine our individual inheritances—we can emphasize tradition and honor and accept the blessings of our heritage, trust in our ancestors' faith, study their experiences, and think about their lives and the good gifts they have passed down to us and which of those gifts we want to pass to our own descendants. These things help us create a connection that can help us hold on, allowing others to lift us up.

Isaac, Madeleine, and Emily

Let me give you an example of the strength of the chain. Polygamy and stories of Joseph Smith's plural marriages in Nauvoo or Brigham Young's in Utah can be troubling—unsettling at best and testimony breakers at the worst. Loggers use these stories constantly to cut down trees of faith. I know those faith-shaking feelings and fears. Personally, I wish we'd never had plural marriage. Yet I am a descendent of such unions. On my father's side I am the sixth link in the gospel chain. The Farleys were in Nauvoo before the Saints, when it was named Commerce. They joined the Church, then endured persecutions, the Martyrdom, Winter Quarters, and the long, hard journey to the Salt Lake Valley. Isaac Farley was a boy at the time of migration.

The family moved to Ogden, and Isaac later fell in love with a convert from Italy named Madeleine Malan. He was twenty-one; she was eighteen. He proposed, and she accepted. They loved each other. They went to Salt Lake City to be married, but when Brigham Young learned Madeleine had a twin sister, named Emily, he told the couple to return to Ogden and bring Emily. He would then seal both sisters to Isaac. I wonder what Madeleine and Isaac talked of as they rode back to Ogden. Isaac proposed to Emily, and the three returned to Salt Lake, where Brigham Young married them. They were obedient believers. At the time Isaac was the youngest man to enter into plural marriage. Of course, I don't know what conversations were had between Isaac, Madeleine, and Brigham Young or the ones with Emily. They all may have felt fine about the situation, but when I read this story, I can't help thinking that Brigham Young was a bit too presumptive, to say the least, and, to my twenty-first-century mindset, too controlling and authoritarian. Different times!

The situation was difficult. Isaac had two families to support, and all three had hard, long days of labor. Both sisters bore children. After eleven years as a plural wife, Emily was approached by a man named Myron Abbot, who promised to take better care of her. She divorced Isaac and married Myron, but the marriage proved unhappy. Emily, remembering life with Isaac and Madeleine, divorced again and was resealed to Isaac. She was a strong woman, as was Madeleine. I honor them. Isaac later spent six months in the state penitentiary in 1887 and 1888 after being arrested for cohabitation.

Isaac, Madeleine, and Emily are buried together in the Ogden City Cemetery. Standing by their graves and pondering their lives is a sobering, reverent experience. I wonder how they did it. I admit some may find some elements in their story to be troubling. My sympathy embraces all three individuals, but I also wonder what they knew. What experiences, what moments with the Spirit instilled in them enduring courage and conviction? In many ways they weren't part of the "standard" family, though their experiences are representative of other plural marriages. They may not have been the ideal Latter-day Saint family. They had their struggles—many I am sure they never shared with their posterity. There may have been times they doubted their faith. I have often wondered and pondered how they held on and remained such committed Church members. I love them for their examples and continually draw strength from them. They were stayers! Section 86-ers! They chose for me! God bless them for it!

I stand in the sealing room, looking in the mirrors, and see the three of them several links back in the reflections. I feel their hearts turn to me and their sympathy with my struggles. I feel their strength. What would I say to Isaac, Madeleine, and Emily if I followed the impulses to leave because of concerns about the stories, doctrines, and accusations that spring from this practice and period of Latter-day-Saint history? What if I walked away due to an overly assertive leader? I believe my ancestors would understand and hope I would carry forward and honor the good gifts they gave so I could still bestow them onto the following generations. The love I feel from them is eternal, not conditional. Yet I hear them question me and those I talk with who are leaving because of these difficulties—they question not with condemnation, not with judgment, but with gentleness—"You will surrender to this impulse to leave? Your faith is so shaken just reading about our lives? About the prophets we followed—Joseph and Brigham? We lived it and didn't walk!" So we draw strength from the chain. They offer experience, belief, commitment, and love down through the generations.

"The Prayer in the Heart of Thy Mother"

There are multiple chains from which we can derive united strength. All of us, whether a part of the first or the eighth generation in the gospel, share the heritage of those early Saints who sacrificed so much to give us all we enjoy both temporally and spiritually. When I was sealed to Laurie, each generation linking the reflections behind her became mine and those behind me became hers. We forged a chain between two families. On my mother's side I am the fourth generation of Church members. Anders Jensen helped a boy being beaten in the streets of Copenhagen for being a member of the Church. Anders was given a tract containing Joseph Smith's story and believed it after the first reading. Though persecution and alienation followed, he held firm, married a poor Swedish girl named Bernadine Dok, had several children, then left for Utah, where he worked to earn money to bring his family over. Even in Utah he faced opposition, being constantly called, "the immigrant."

Anders and Bernadine gave me my nation and my faith. They were the genesis seeds that produced their granddaughter, my mother. How would I answer them if I gave in to the impulses to leave? In their expansive Danish hearts, I suppose they would say, "Well, Michael, find where you can do the most good and stand there." I do not think they would want me to feel shame in my decision. Yet, I sense there would be an ache in their souls. I once spoke with a young mother who had left the Church. She talked of the chain in her life. I felt the poignancy of her decision when she said, "I think of this often with my grandmother. Would she be proud of me? I hope so. I feel like I'm still a good person." That brought me to tears for she *was* a good person.

Growing up, my mother would say to my sisters and me, "All I want is 100 percent!" We knew she was referring to having a continual commitment to the Savior, His gospel, and the Church she loved and served. As we married and had children of our own she took each grandchild and said to them, "All I want is 100 percent!" They grew, married, and had their own families. Once again—when old and limited in energy but loved by her growing posterity—each great-grandchild heard those same intense, hopeful words. She died a few years ago. I see her in temple mirrors watching us, as she told us she would, until we join her and give her what she most desired in life. There is strength in the chain! I imagine myself meeting my mother again behind the veil and what I will say to her. I want to draw on her convictions and hopes—they are a part of me. Drawing on the strength of the chain and the gifts my family has given me helps me put aside the insensitive, troubling leaders and face the faith-shaking challenges, knowing that I am not alone.

I look at the chain in the temple mirrors, and the final two sentences of my patriarchal blessing come to mind. One speaks of ancestors and posterity, the fulfillment of promises and a future reunion "with them in the Resurrection of the righteous with the hand of fellowship, love and great rejoicing together." The other refers to my mother, who sat in the room and wept when she heard it: "I bless thee with the power to walk the strait and narrow path, seeking to fulfill the prayer that shall always be in the heart of thy mother." Great anchors of my soul!

CHAPTER SEVEN

CENTER THE ESSENTIALS

In memory of our God,
our religion, and freedom,
and our peace, our wives,
and our children.

—Alma 46:12

Faith and Family

On the plains and hills of Transylvania in Romania are some exceptionally interesting churches. They're not beautiful cathedrals, just simple village chapels, but they leave a lasting impression. Dating from the thirteenth to the sixteenth centuries, they once numbered above 300, and more than 150 still exist. Labeled "fortified churches" because of a tight, protective wall that encircles each one, they seem too big for their enclosures—bell towers peak over the tops of the walls, dominating the landscape. The shielding walls are high and many feet thick. They were originally built by German settlers colonizing the area north and west of the Carpathian Mountains by the invitation of Hungarian kings. This region was constantly under threat from the Ottoman Turks, who launched waves of invasions in the area.

Villagers needed places of refuge to withstand attacks and sieges that recurred as constant as the seasons. Churches, the center of their communities, were protected with forethought. And the German settlers did even more! Inside a number of the walls surrounding the churches, small apartments were built for families to live in during times of danger. These settlers identified what they considered most necessary to defend and built accordingly. Two things, and only two, were decisively essential to them—faith and family. I don't believe there is anything I could say that equals the visual power of these fortified churches and villages. We too can counter dangers, the impulses to leave, by centering the essentials—faith and family.

I was raised by my mother alone. Due to painful experiences, challenges, and choices weighing on my father, he followed the impulses to leave even though he had been instrumental in bringing my mother to her own committed testimony. It was not a matter of doubt or offenses, of historical or scriptural unease, but one of lifestyle. My father always believed. He loved the faith in which he was raised. He came from pioneer stock. Belief was natural in him. Yet forces in his life made it difficult for him to remain in a Church environment. He left my mother, my sisters, and me. A divorce followed when I was still a baby, and my father moved to Utah while my mother stayed in California. I knew very little of him growing up, though my mother always spoke positively about him. My father was a gifted and talented man. When I reached my late teens and attended Brigham Young University, I forged a close relationship with him, and he became an integral part of my life—it was one of the best decisions I ever made.

The week of my marriage, I drove from Southern California through Utah, picked up my father, and continued on to Alberta, Canada, where Laurie and I were going to be married in the Cardston Temple. I wanted my father there. Though he didn't have a recommend, he would wait on the grounds outside the temple.

I was anxious to see Laurie after six weeks of separation and didn't want to stop overnight in Salt Lake. My father agreed, and we drove through the night. We had a long, serious talk about his life and choices and my future. I had not invited the conversation, but he was in a pensive mood. After one long, reflective period he said with great earnestness, as well as I can remember, "In a few days you will be married. Nothing is more important than the family you will form and the faith that will guide you. Never lose them!" I stopped the car, and we wept together, then finished the drive—mostly in silence. Laurie and I included my father in every family function we could, from holidays and Sunday dinners to vacations in the popup trailer. After long, hard wrestlings, he returned to activity, served a mission on Temple Square, and in the temple. We had what I call an "Ensign ending," a happy one. He helped me in a circuitous way to center the essentials in my life.

"A Better Cause"

One of the most iconic images in the Book of Mormon is Captain Moroni waving the title of liberty to rally his people to defend what was most essential to them. Just like the German settlers along the Carpathian Mountains, Moroni's people protected the necessities of faith and family. The principles on Moroni's torn coat are repeated nine times in Alma 43 through 48—the single strongest emphasis in the story of the Nephite wars. It seems clear to me that the centering of faith and family, as well as freedom, is the critical lesson and the primary reason for including the "war chapters" in the Book of Mormon. Understanding their relevance comes by applying them to spiritual rather than literal battles.

In the spiritual war being fought today, I have, as

I'm sure some of you do, great concerns for my children, grandchildren, and in the not so distant future, great-grandchildren. I pay close attention to the story of Captain Moroni. It is a story about centering essentials. (In truth much in the Book of Mormon centers on family as an essential.) Mormon writes, "The Nephites were inspired by *a better cause*, . . . they were fighting for their homes and their liberties, their wives and their children, and their all, yea, for their rites of worship and their church" (Alma 43:45, emphasis added). Captain Moroni told the attacking Zerahemnah, "Ye are angry with us because of our religion . . . to which," among other things, "we owe all our happiness" (Alma 44:2, 5). He built "walls of stone to encircle them about. . . . Thus he was preparing to support their liberty, their lands, their wives, and their children, and their peace, and that they might live unto the Lord their God, and that they might maintain that which was called by their enemies *the cause of Christians*" (Alma 48:8, 10, emphasis added). Since Moroni was "a man of a perfect understanding" (Alma 48:11), I assume he knew what causes, what essentials, were worth protecting.

Later in the story, political divisions undermine Moroni's defenses. We see in the narrative of the stripling warriors the compelling, faith-creating influence that parents, especially mothers, have on their children. "They had been taught to believe—that there was a just God" (Alma 57:26). "They had been taught by their mothers. . . . And they rehearsed unto me the words of their mothers, saying: We do not doubt our mothers knew it" (Alma 56:47–48). This scriptural emphasis on family is one thing that makes our faith so influential in our daily lives. As in Book of Mormon times, our modern world needs this same emphasis and the blessings that flow from it.

What's in the Center?

Sometimes we can be sidetracked into areas we perceive as being decisive and vital but come at the sacrifice of faith and family. Remember Mormon's words that the Nephites were inspired by a "*better* cause." There are many causes in the world calling for our support and demanding our energies. Though we wish to maintain, as well as we can, every worthy thing, we must give care. Sometimes distractions, from present movements to personal preferences, shift into the center of our lives and attention, with belief sidelined or rejected altogether. Sometimes, like my father, those distractions concern desired lifestyles. They may be political causes or ideologies. They may be ambitions or goals that don't always harmonize with the ideals upheld by faith. They may be anger over a given offense. They may be feelings, for various reasons, that one does not belong anymore in the Church environment. Believing members of the Church may cause others to feel alienated, or members who leave may at least sense alienation—the inviting, inclusive spirit is either not given openly enough or is not perceived to be given. Either way, faith's blessings at the center, often still loved, are replaced, no longer protectable—no longer available for the families inside the walls.

Differences can have threatening, center-shifting power. Our personal opinions or positions may be so intense that when others, or the Church as an institution, do not agree with us, barriers become wider than they need be or contention develops. Nothing is so tempting as moral indignation! People putting their personal agendas at the center can be found among the very religious as well as the disaffected. We often want others to think as we do because we are convinced we are right. I dearly love Lincoln's second inaugural address, in which he tried to bring the nation together by saying, "With malice for none; with charity for all; with firmness in the right, as *God gives us to see the right*, let us strive on to finish the work we are in; to bind up the nation's wounds" (*The Living Lincoln: The Man and His Times, in His Own Words*, edited by Paul M. Angle and Earl Schenck Miers [New York: Barnes and Noble, 1955], 640, emphasis added). We should emulate that touch of humility, so typical of Lincoln, that modest element of uncertainty that our firmness in the right *is* right, and the hope God will help us see where we need to make adjustments. *Right*, with a capital *R*, is a delicate, searched-for end—reasoned or revealed— but not always best determined by popular public sentiment, biblical interpretations, congressional laws, or historical traditions. We do the best we can to think and live right, but maintaining that touch of humility is helpful, in all areas of life—religious, political, moral, and scientific.

And of course, at the center of our lives should be the necessary "charity for all"—charity that can "bind up . . . wounds." Joseph Smith wrote of the need for this expansive, inclusive love while suffering in Liberty Jail.

> We ought always to be aware of those prejudices which sometimes so strangely present themselves, and are so congenial to human nature, against our friends, neighbors, and brethren of the world, who choose to differ from us in opinion and in matters of faith. . . . There is a love from God that should be exercised toward those of our faith, who walk uprightly, which is peculiar to itself, but it is without prejudice; it also gives scope to the mind, which enables us to conduct ourselves with greater liberality towards all that are not of our faith, than what they exercise towards

one another. These principles approximate nearer to the mind of God, because it is like God. ("History, 1838–1856, volume C-1 [2 November 1838–31 July 1842]," 911, josephsmithpapers.org)

Charity for all!

There is room under the gospel tent for disagreements and diversities of opinion without uprooting the center and abandoning goodness, truth, and doctrines upon which we share common ground. I was singularly impressed with one fortified church. It was originally built as a Catholic church, but with the Reformation the Saxon settlers became Lutheran and converted the church accordingly. Yet inside the defensive wall a small chapel for Catholic villagers was built. Within the protective walls, the people accommodated different beliefs. There were also Muslim prayer rugs hanging on the inside of many of the churches—gifts from returning merchants who traded in the Middle East.

I once had a frank conversation with an independent-thinking young woman who had some issues with the Church, and I asked, "What would push you over the edge?" She answered, "The less I am made to feel I need to conform to a certain mold, the more I am willing to stay. I will never be a geometric shape!" We laughed at her analogy, but I admire her desire to contribute with her

God-given strengths—one of which was a questing, open, and independent mind. We need her!

Most disheartening is the loss of religious belief altogether. Following the impulses to leave can mean leaving everything. We may create this problem by asserting too strongly that it is all or nothing. People do leave the Church and remain devoted Christians. Jesus is still their center. I am personally less distressed when those I know leave but engage in another faith. Most discouraging is to see people without faith or belief of any kind. They remain good, decent people—please don't misunderstand—but faith not only ceases to take a central place in their lives, it takes no place at all. If we follow the impulses to leave, the question should always be asked, "What is in the center now? Will it hold the orbit of my life?" I can withstand interruptions to my rejoicing or the injuries inflicted by others because I don't know anything quite as good to put in the center than the gospel, scripture, the Savior, the many really worthy people, the doctrines of the Restoration, and so on. What if nothing replaces them? What if there were no center to draw on or focus our lives? No spiritual essentials?

"Living" and "Good"

There are phrases and terms used in the Church that are used so much, they sometimes seem to lose a great deal of meaning and force. The standard testimony phrase is "I know this Church is true." It is a perfectly fine thing to say, but suppose we didn't have that expression? The phrase in the Doctrine and Covenants is actually "true and living church" (Doctrine and Covenants 1:30). *Living* is a grand word! It suggests growth, change, adaptation, movement, correction, and increasing maturity. It suggests the quickening presence of the Spirit. The word is a perfect reflection of just what the Church has done over the years. It grows! Not only in numbers and reach but also in understanding and awareness. What if we said, "I know this Church is living"? For me this statement has vitality and immediacy that is comforting. Faith in the center is *living* faith.

Sometimes I eliminate other expressions or words often used to see how I can replace them. For example, we use the word *Atonement* a great deal to cover almost everything. I love the word, but if we didn't have it, how would we describe what the Savior does for us? We invite fresh insight. What could be another way to say "true"? Teaching the poor Zoramites, Alma compared the word to a seed planted in the heart. If it was "a true seed, or a good seed," it would grow and begin to produce spiritual, emotional, behavioral, and intellectual effects (Alma 32:28). What I find interesting is that Alma drops the word *true* and relies only on the word *good* to describe how one knows God is in the growing seed. He used *good*, and only *good*, a dozen times. Goodness was the means of perceiving God's presence—goodness reveals truth.

We may overemphasize the word *truth* as the only qualifier, but goodness is powerful, often more readily perceived in religious matters, and more openly inclusive. There is such goodness in the doctrines, emphasis on Christ, hopes and aspirations, programs, leadership, scriptures, history, and ordinances of The Church of Jesus Christ of Latter-day Saints. It is this goodness that holds the center, encircling and blessing families. If wrestling with the question "Is it true?" it may be helpful to put that question on the shelf for a season and simply ask, "Is it good?" This question focuses us, as Alma desired, on the fruits of faith—fruits "most precious" and "sweet above all that is sweet" (Alma 32:42).

There is another strategy for keeping family-blessing faith at the center. In Fyodor Dostoyevsky's great novel *The Brothers Karamazov*, the beloved Father Zosima of the Russian Orthodox Church discusses the loss of belief with a woman wanting to recover her childhood faith in God. "How, how am I to restore my faith?" she pleads. "How can it be proven, how can one be convinced it is true?" His answer is somewhat unexpected, but I think it is one of the greatest answers to those questions. It focuses on goodness. "Here it is not possible to prove anything; it is however, possible to be convinced. . . . By the experience of active love. Try to love your fellow human beings actively and untiringly. In the degree to which you succeed in that love, you will also be convinced of God's existence. . . . And if you attain complete self-renunciation in your love for your fellow creatures, then you will unfailingly come to believe, and no form of doubt will ever be able to visit your soul. That has been tested, that is precisely true" (*The Brothers Karamazov*, translated by David McDuff [New York: Penguin Books, 1993], 60).

Here we are not just examining goodness but acting it out, creating it through love, and with the creation, faith in God follows. Goodness and faith are bound together in the center. Sometimes it is best to lay aside wrestlings, doubts, minute examinations of beliefs, or the people who espouse them and just serve, just love, just forgive, just practice goodness and see it in others. I believe that is what "come unto Christ" means. To those experiencing center-altering emotions, George MacDonald counseled: "Fold the arms of thy faith, and wait in quietness until light goes up in thy darkness. Fold the arms of thy Faith I say, but not of thy Action: bethink thee of something that thou oughtest to do, and go and do it" (*Unspoken Sermons* [Charleston, SC: Bibliobazaar, 2006], 89).

By placing our Savior, the gospel, goodness, the Church, and family as essentials in the center, we find a wonderful arena in which to "do thy work" (Doctrine and Covenants 109:33). We offer Dostoyevsky's selfless service and love. Using gifts given to us by God, we spread their benefits. We may believe we do not need the Church, but that is not the real question. *We* are needed! We participate to give, not just to receive, and all have something to share, both within the Church and the broader world. Even our questions can be a gift. What we receive is the bonus, and it comes from many quarters. That is mature religion!

The Center of the Center

There is a center of the center, the essential of the essentials. If it holds strong, most faith crises are borne, interruptions overcome, and purposeful loggers resisted. If it gives way or is lost, the rest becomes nearly impossible to sustain. It was the staple of Jesus's life. It is the constant, deeply personal, open, pouring-out, holding-nothing-back communication with the Father and the accompanying desire of doing only that which pleases Him. Jesus came to teach us this.

Prayer is another word I sometimes pretend I don't

have and look for alternatives. We *wrestle, supplicate, cry out, hunger, fill with desire, labor, adore*—choose the words that mean most to you. *Pour out* is my favorite. In chapter 3, we looked at Joseph Smith's affirmation that we must "commune with God" ("History, 1838–1856, volume C-1 [2 November 1838–31 July 1842]," 904[b], josephsmith-papers.org). Of everything my mother taught me, I am most grateful for learning I could talk to my Father in Heaven about all things, anywhere, all the time. He is our dearest friend, the Whispering One, who doesn't need to talk loudly because He is near. There is no bewilderment, doubt, or anxiety I haven't shared with Him; no troubling episode in my own life, injury landed on my soul by others, or concern with the Church, its history or position on an issue of which He is not aware—not because of His omniscience but because I tell Him. He listens even when I question His running of the world, occasionally bordering on accusation. This "pouring out" has made all the difference in my life. To those who may have left, I say, I believe God is bigger than any single religion. We may leave a particular faith, but He does not leave us nor must we think we are leaving Him. Keep the conversation alive.

The Apostle Paul once stood on Mars Hill in Athens surrounded by the great contributions to learning and human endeavor that Athens's curious questing spirit brought to the world: democracy, philosophy, art, architecture, theater, medicine, literature, sport, and half a dozen other areas of wisdom and achievement. In that enriching Mecca of human attainment, he added one more necessary aspiration of a civilized, cultured people, of all people at any level of development—the "feeling after God" until we "find him." This quest is an individual one. Paul taught that finding God is not as difficult as we may believe, for "he be not far from every one of us." This was the one thing among every other excellence that "all nations of men" who "dwell on all the face of the earth . . . should seek" (Acts 17:26–27). If we find Him and never stop talking with Him, we can get through all things.

I have laid every challenge on my faith's journey on the altar of God. Just placing it there is relieving. If the challenge is doubting the existence of Him to whom one is talking, keep the conversation alive even if it feels one-sided. That is all we can do. We then leave it in God's hands to help us feel His reality. This is what a Lamanite king did as he struggled to find faith in a God he did not know. "O God," King Laman prayed, "Aaron hath told me that there is a God; and if thou art God, wilt thou make thyself known unto me, and I will give away all my sins to know thee" (Alma 22:18). The sincere willingness to do whatever necessary is the great revealing poignancy of this prayer.

My first experience with the temple endowment was, to say the least, a traumatic one. I was totally unprepared. I was bewildered, frightened, confused, filled with doubt, overpowered with anxiety—and to be truly honest, I walked away from the temple saying, "This cannot be part of my church!" I didn't know how to find meaning in the symbols, so all was alien. I thought maybe there was something wrong with me that I couldn't just believe and feel peace. Had I been older, more settled, and more secure in my own wisdom, perhaps the impulses to leave would have been strong enough at that moment to shift the essentials out of my center. What a world of fulfillment and joy I would have missed. I could not return to the temple again until after my mission. During the intervening time I talked about it all with my Father in Heaven. Those conversations and my mother's faith were the constants of my life. I could pour it all out and feel His reassurance that all would be well. It was another "hold on" contingency. In time and with spiritual maturity, the meaning and beauty of sacred ordinances opened up to me until I loved the temple. Until that happened, love and trust in a listening God held faith in the center of my life. This was the ledge to which I clung.

Really communing in a deeply personal and honest way with our Father in Heaven eases the impulses to leave and walk away. As long as those conversations continue; as long as we talk about our difficulties, doubts, questions, offenses, fears, disillusionments, and even embitterment—as long as we persist in speaking with a listening God, we can keep loved and cherished beliefs in the center. This is the one permanent, unremitting element in life that bequeaths staying power. When I was young, Mother took me to see Bryce Canyon National Park. I was awed, stunned by the beauty. The reverent silence was overpowering. I knew there was a God, not for the splendor alone but for the feeling inside me that could be touched and moved by it. I believed I could talk with the Being that put such sensitivity into me and that He wanted me to respond to Him in the same manner as I did to His creations.

The *Lectures on Faith* teach the power of human testimony, how it "stirred up the faith of multitudes to feel after [God]—to search after a knowledge of his character, perfections and attributes, until they became extensively acquainted with him, and not only commune with him and behold his glory, but be partakers of his power and stand in his presence." This inquiry "always terminated when rightly pursued, in the most glorious discoveries and eternal certainty" (*Lectures on Faith* [1985], 34, 56). Eternal certainty is the aim of our quest, but it runs through communion with, searching for, and feeling after the Father, knowing His attributes. It is how the Restoration started and the only way it can be maintained both in individual lives and the overall Church.

Several weeks after initially visiting the fortified churches in Romania, I returned a second time to feel anew their visual power. I'd love to take all members of the Church there and let them see and feel what I saw and felt. They instilled in me a fervent desire, a committed, renewed determination to maintain faith and family securely within protective walls—to center the essentials.

BENEDICTION

One of the earliest lessons impressed on my soul was the need to be a "stayer." The experience was a vital tutorial impacting multiple areas of my life. It did not involve anything so consequential or soul wrenching as leaving a religion, but it taught me lessons that I have been able to apply to more serious concerns of life. I return to an early spring day in Southern California. I hear the hissing of a baseball across home plate as I miss it again. I was twelve or thirteen. Baseball was my first love. I dreamed it, hungered for it, played it every free minute—almost worshipped it. God Himself, I was sure, had created baseball and probably on the first day, right after light.

I had hit the ball well at tryouts and was chosen for the Little League team I wanted. But now? I don't know why I couldn't hit the ball that day. It was just a practice. Nothing hung on the outcome of my connecting bat to ball. The coach was pitching. Maybe he wanted to teach me something with each curve or slider. Maybe my confidence had waned, replaced with growing fear and doubt. I only know I could not hit the ball. My best friend was sitting behind the backstop. I could sense his anxiety and growing embarrassment—then his empathy. Still the ball came on and on in an agony of silence admitting only that serpent hiss of stitched leather across air, not the cracking sound of connection that thrilled me. I struck out at least half a dozen times that day. The coach stopped the painful hurling of the ball and held it in his hand. I sensed his disappointment and felt completely demoralized. I dropped the bat across home plate and started walking away. I didn't hear anyone encourage me to come back, though they likely did.

I was mad at the coach, at the team, at my friend who quietly said to me as I passed him, "I sure wish you had hit it once." Unfortunately, I let that momentary failure determine my future course. I turned my back on baseball, and no amount of pleading ever brought me back. My belief in the game, in my desire to play it and master it, leaked out of me on that long walk home and during my conversation with my mother as I told her, "I don't want to play Little League anymore." Yet, during that same walk, I heard another voice in my head urging me to turn around, to stay, to remain and try again, not to give up, not to walk! The love and joy that had been part of my life as long as I could remember would return! The present disenchantment, even resentment, anger, and blame would fade! The old feeling would come back! This was only an interruption! I think it was the voice of the grown Michael Wilcox talking to his young self, knowing that for the rest of his life he would regret that last dropping of the bat. But I was a boy, and what did I know of that future man's heart and wisdom?

It was that same year, or close to it, that I walked a second time. My mother wanted her children to gain a musical talent. It was important to her, and she sacrificed part of her single-mother teacher's salary to acquaint us with the joys of music. One older sister took voice lessons. My other sister and I sat before white and black keys and set about mastering the piano. Scales, practice, and mini recitals pressed down on me like a weight. I came up with every argument and reason why this was not what I wanted or needed. My mother persisted, but in time I wore her out and she relented. The lessons and practice ceased. I remember the rush of initial freedom I felt at this walking away, much different than the baseball episode. I was relieved and happy. In time I picked up a guitar and played it for a few years. But music was essentially out of my life. Yet within the initial release I also felt a vague discomfort. Minimal at first, it grew over the months and then years. I heard the voice again telling me, "Stay!" Each time I passed a piano, the sense I had left something desirable rose in me—not enough to return me to the piano bench but sufficient to bring a twinge of regret. Now many years and decades later, my disappointment over not being a "stayer," a "remainer," only increases. I never see a piano without feeling that unease.

Maybe I got all the walking away out of me at age twelve or thirteen. I hope so. Maybe the memories, conscious or unconscious, forged an unknown need to never walk away from something worthwhile again—to fight the impulses to leave. I want to be a "stayer," a "sticker," an "endurer," a "continuer," a "remainer." I want to stand and "be not moved" (Doctrine and Covenants 87:8). I haven't always been as steady and consistent as I would like, but the desire is constant. It is something we choose by an active volition of will. There is dignity in holding on. We see this in so many areas of living, from personal relationships to educational goals. This desire causes some of us to finish the book we are not that interested in, or the hike to the mountaintop when we would rather take the easy trail back down. It makes us stick out the seemingly unnecessary courses leading to a degree rather than quit school and just get a job. (I think I would have quit school, I disliked it so, if I could have and just lived on the ranch with the horses, cattle, sweat, and cool evenings by the river.) I believe the need to be a stayer is never so critical as in the religious atmosphere of our lives.

Often I hear the *eternal* Michael Wilcox's voice entreating the *mortal* Michael to fight the impulses to leave. That eternal Michael is so very much wiser than the mortal one. God uses every experience of our lives to teach and prepare us for eternity—even failure on a Little League baseball field or the mere passing of a piano. So in the context of my life and my chosen faith, I tell myself I must remain with my beliefs, with my heritage, with the spiritual things in my soul, with the memories, the people, the goodness, the beauty, the truths, the past experiences—which all together produced me and continue to urge me to progress. Above all, I want my God and my Savior at the center of my life.

Dante expressed his faith with ascending verbs defining ever-increasing assurance of all he hoped for in his journey from mortality to eternity. "Thus I believe, thus I affirm, thus I am certain it is . . ." (as quoted by Robert Browning; see *Letters of Robert Browning*, edited by Thurman L. Hood [New Haven: Yale University Press, 1933], 171). I love that rise of conviction. The things of the soul move through belief, affirmation, and certitude.

They also fluctuate as we live and experience challenges, opposition, and resistance. We try to stay on the stairway of those three words and not slip into, "Thus I doubt, thus I deny, thus I am convinced it is not so." This journey is and has been, for me, lifelong. Belief and trust are acceptable. It doesn't always have to be, "I know . . ." Jesus told Thomas, who wanted the certain-it-is testimony, "Blessed are they that have not seen, and yet have believed" (John 20:29). Even if we reach near certainty in matters of faith, the desire for constant assurance never goes away, as Shakespeare wrote, "For truth can never be confirmed enough, though doubts did ever sleep" (*Pericles*, Act V, Scene II, 203–4).

We may not have strong belief or certainty in all things, but we can hold on to those things we do believe while we pour out our thoughts to the Lord, asking for faith and strength in those things where we still wrestle or struggle. Yet when honest doubts come—or impulses to leave tempt us—we can be prepared! We can be "stayers." I am strengthened by words from Theodore Roosevelt, applicable to all who struggle—against the impulses to leave not only our faith but anything worthy behind: "It is not the critic who counts; not the man who points out how the strong man stumbles, or where the doer of deeds could have done them better. The credit belongs to the man who is actually in the arena, whose face is marred by dust and sweat and blood; who strives valiantly; who errs, who comes short again and again, because there is no effort without error and shortcoming; but who does actually strive to do the deeds; who knows great enthusiasms, the great devotions; who spends himself in a worthy cause" ("Citizen in a Republic," speech, Sorbonne, Paris, April 23, 1910).

To those in the arena, my heart is with you, and your Father in Heaven is with you and understands. "Father, help us face those impulses to leave while we continue holding on!"

May 18, 2020

ABOUT THE AUTHOR

S. MICHAEL WILCOX received his PhD from the University of Colorado and taught for many years at the Church's Institute of Religion adjacent to the University of Utah. He has spoken to packed crowds at BYU Education Week and has hosted tours to the Holy Land, to China, to Church history sites, and beyond. Michael has also served in a variety of callings, including as a bishop and a counselor in a stake presidency. He has written many articles and books, including *House of Glory, Sunset, 10 Great Souls I Want to Meet in Heaven, Twice Blessed, Finding Hope,* and *What Seek Ye?* He and his late wife, Laurie, are the parents of five children.